The question is not *if* we will suffer in this life, but rather, how we build resilient souls and nurture a durable hope when we inevitably face suffering. Beginning with his own powerful example, each of the true stories in Jeff Munroe's *Telling Stories in the Dark* model for us all a path toward a redemptive stewardship of pain that we would do well to ponder, pursue, and proclaim to others.

Jeff Crosby, author of *The Language of the Soul: Meeting God in the Longings of our Hearts*

Jeff Munroe is a masterful storyteller, brilliantly weaving together the compelling real-life stories of individuals who've been wounded by tragedy with experts' commentary on how to find insight, hope, and healing from each narrative. We all experience deep loss at some point in our lives, and *Telling Stories in the Dark* is a rich contemplation on navigating trauma and grief.

Karen Mulder, founder of the Wisdom of the Wounded ministry

At the core of the Christian mystery is the notion of redemptive suffering, how brokenness becomes beatitude and grief is transformed by grace, how gratitude inoculates against our grievances. Jeff Munroe identifies the power of telling our own stories—sharing our experience, strength, and hopes—as the *passe-partout* for our spiritual journey: life's master-key.

Thomas Lynch, poet and author of *The Undertaking* **and** *Bone Rosary*

Jeffrey Munroe has written an unusual book. It is hard to classify, which is one of its strengths. He tells "stories in the dark," stories of suffering in all of their anguishing and horrible variety. He writes with grace, elegance, and empathy. However painful, the stories have a strange beauty to them. As he puts it, he is trying to "play" with pain. It sounds irreverent. It is in fact the opposite. But he also reflects on those stories, often by interacting with professionals who provide a larger perspective, about trauma, forgiveness, injustice, and more. It is this combination of powerful stories and deep, insightful reflection on those stories that makes this book so moving, compelling, and informative. I read it in one sitting. It drew me in, kept me there, and captivated me.

Gerald L. Sittser, professor emeritus of theology, Whitworth University, and author of *A Grace Disguised*

Jeff Munroe avoids the quicksand of theodicy to focus instead on the stories of people whose faith has survived great suffering, which he tells with warmth, generosity, and compassion.

Christian Wiman, author of *My Bright Abyss: Meditations of a Modern Believer*. Professor of the Practice of Religion and Literature, Yale Divinity School

In John 16, Jesus tells his disciples, "In this world you will face trouble," and he's right. We will. Jeffrey Munroe does not shy away from the suffering in the world, but instead invites the reader to explore stories of pain and suffering in a way that shines a light in the darkness. I would recommend this book to anyone who is presently suffering or is suffering-adjacent. In other words: This book is for everyone.

April Fiet, author of *The Sacred Pulse: Holy Rhythms for Overwhelmed Souls*

Telling Stories in the Dark is powerful and memorable. Jeffrey Munroe tells stories of people's pain and grief in a way that is sensitive, wise and at times raw, eloquent and searingly honest, theologically and psychologically sophisticated, and ultimately redemptive. It's a book about loss—and a book about healing and hope. Jeff Munroe has been a good steward of his pain, and a good steward of the pain of others. *Telling Stories in the Dark* is a needed gift to a broken world.

Peter Wehner, Senior Fellow at The Trinity Forum, Contributing Writer to *The Atlantic* and *The New York Times*

Jeff Munroe's *Telling Stories in the Dark* takes very seriously Frederick Buechner's dictum to reflect on our "stewardship of pain." With grace and truth, he narrates his own story and the stories of others to ponder suffering and a faithful response to it. You'll definitely be blessed to spend time with Jeff and his friends!

Jennifer L. Holberg, author of *Nourishing Narratives: The Power of Story to Shape Our Faith*. Professor and Chair, Department of English, Calvin University; Co-Director, Calvin Center for Faith & Writing

Jeffrey Munroe's book reflects and expands on the ground-breaking work of Harold Kushner's *When Bad Things Happen to Good People*—exploring the problem of evil and how it can exist in our world with an omnipotent and omniscient God. Addressing this timeless question in a fresh way, Munroe has compiled true stories of resilience and hope amid great suffering. Readers are graced with the intimate conversations and dilemmas of individuals, couples, families, and communities who honestly and openly share their pain, tragedy, and triumph.

Readers will be transformed by these physical, existential, spiritual, and communal experiences. Among the accounts are stories of trauma, grace, and ultimately resilience in the wake of physical injury, gun violence, cancer, medical mistakes, racial misunderstanding, and so much more. A noteworthy gift of the book is the conversations in which Munroe analyzes these stories with relevant experts to discuss and interpret the tragedies and triumphs. This process gives readers lots of practical advice and transformative nuggets of truth. I even enjoyed a few heart-healing poems Munroe includes.

As we read and become a part of this storytelling, Jeffrey Munroe's circle becomes a guardian of our collective personhood.

Micah L. McCreary, President of New Brunswick Theological Seminary and author of *Trauma and Race: A Path to Wellbeing*

Telling Stories in the Dark

Finding healing and hope in sharing
our sadness, grief, trauma, and pain

Jeffrey Munroe

Foreword by Sarah Arthur

For more information and further discussion, visit:

ReformedJournal.com

A free discussion guide is available at:

ReformedJournal.com/books

For those whose stories are told in these pages,
and for those whose stories still need to be told.

Contents

A story is what makes us real.

Wright Thompson

Foreword

My video interview with Jeff Munroe happened on the worst possible day.

I'd just lost my hair. My tongue felt chalky. My face oozed with hundreds of tiny pustules. The first round of chemo had been just a few weeks prior, and already the side-effects felt more dehumanizing (if possible) than the cancer diagnosis itself. The last thing I wanted was to be on camera.

But I trusted Jeff.

We'd met a few years earlier when I'd led a workshop during a writing conference at his seminary. He'd been the gracious host, welcoming speakers and attendees alike with joyful humility. His deep love for great writing, for stories, for the humanity of the storytellers, added dignity and depth to what, on any other campus, could've been a cerebral academic summit.

Later, when he learned I was writing a book called *A Light So Lovely: The Spiritual Legacy of Madeleine L'Engle, Author of A Wrinkle in Time*, he reached out regarding a future interview for his seminary's vlog. No problem! I thought. After eleven published titles, PR came easy. Plus, the book's release was months away. Plenty of time to prepare.

But then—six hours after I turned in the book's final edits—I received news. Stage one breast cancer. Aggressive, high-risk, luminal type B. I'd need surgery followed by chemo followed by five-to-ten years of medication and monitoring. When I should've been celebrating the book's anticipated release, instead I was lying (awake!) in an operating room as a surgeon deftly threaded a PICC line through a vein in my arm to my heart. Chemo began four days after the book hit the shelves.

It can take a few weeks for side-effects to appear, my oncologist warned. The poison can damage follicles, glands, soft tissue. That's when your hair might fall out. Eyebrows and eyelashes, too. Your sense of taste and smell can change. Expect nausea. Don't plan on traveling far.

So I reached out to Jeff. "I probably won't be able to come for the interview, after all," I said. "I'm really sorry."

"Don't worry," he replied. "We'll come to you."

"Really?" My voice wobbled. "Because I don't know how I'll feel. I might have to cancel at the last minute."

"It's okay," he reassured me. "One day at a time."

When we got off the phone, I cried.

Grace wasn't something I'd given myself much of during my own seminary years. I'd welcomed the rigors of academia, the push and challenge of intellectual debate. Theological discourse was a rarified skill at which I excelled. I much preferred to step out of the fray, *talk* about God and life and faith rather than *experience* any of it. Who had time for embodiment? Not me.

Some of this was my temperament. But much of it was learned behavior after years in Reformed (and Reformed-adjacent) circles, which prized the robust life of the mind. Theological orthodoxy was lauded over habituated ortho-praxy: mind over matter. And

I'd embraced it all. My unspoken mantra was *I think, therefore I am saved.*

But then I took a course in post-liberal theology. The work of scholar George Lindbeck, in particular, challenged many of my assumptions. What if the foundation of faith isn't a set of beliefs but, rather, a communal way of life that includes, among other practices, storytelling? After all, without embodied behaviors such as worship, scripture, prayer, sacraments, song, caregiving, preaching, liturgy, narrative, fasting, and celebration, theology has nothing to talk *about.*

Thus, the practices of faith are considered "first-order discourse." They're the foundation, embedded in the life of the community: in its cultural identity, its muscle-memory. They encompass a range of emotions—joy, lament, courage, empathy, rage, guilt, wonder—and touch upon all five senses: taste, touch, sight, smell, sound. They exist *a priori*, before theology has the chance to open its mouth, and will continue long after the last word of the last doctrine has been defined. They reach us on a deeper level than mere intellect, touching the heart, memory, imagination, and soul. Which is why they aren't easily forgotten.

I'm reminded of the difference between C. S. Lewis's cerebral arguments in *The Problem of Pain* versus his journal-like memoir *A Grief Observed*. In the former, the iconic Oxford don walks us through a tidy theological explanation of suffering. In the latter, the new widower bleeds his deeply personal agony all over the pages. In the former, I was dazzled by the clarity of his rhetoric— but, to be honest, I remember little else about it. It's the practice of lament—of expressing sadness and rage—in *A Grief Observed* which grabs me and digs unforgettably into my soul.

Enter *Telling Stories in the Dark*.

Jeff can theologize with the best of them, as his reflections at the end of each chapter will attest. He can fully engage in second-order discourse by which we love the Lord our God with all our minds. But that's not his starting point.

As one who has suffered much—first, through his wife's life-altering stroke mere weeks before their wedding; and, more recently, through a cancer diagnosis of his own—he knows the value of primary Christian practices. Before any theologizing can happen, we offer space for lament. We bring casseroles. We weep with those who weep. We tell stories in the dark. These are the embodied behaviors that shape us into the kinds of people whose way of life speaks louder than any doctrine we profess.

The day Jeff interviewed me, I was at a low point. I sat on stage feeling like I should say something profound. But, in true Jeff fashion, that's not where he started. With the camera rolling, he began by displaying a selection of hats he'd brought, to match the wrap I wore. He joked about his own "male-pattern baldness." Then, with the kindness of an empath, he invited me to tell my story. Not the story of my L'Engle book—although we'd get to that—but my personal story. Of suffering. Of lament. Of a faith that finds itself in the dark.

Here in these pages, that's what you'll find. Story after story of those who walk a similar road. Conversations with those who suffer about how they do—or don't—experience the God who promises never to leave us nor forsake us. Before intellectually exploring any of his chosen topics, Jeff embeds those topics in the lived reality of ordinary people on their worst possible days.

Because this is where God meets us.

And we're invited to join God there.

Sarah Arthur is a breast cancer survivor and the author of twelve nonfiction books about the intersection of faith and great stories. Her thirteenth book, *Once a Queen: A Novel*, kicks off her debut fantasy series for young adults. Visit Sarah online at: www.saraharthur.com

I

'Let Me Tell You a Story'

"If we do not transform our pain, we will most surely transmit it."
Father Richard Rohr, Franciscan priest

"To truly laugh, you must take your pain and play with it!"
Charlie Chaplin

"I cannot solve that puzzle—but let me tell you a story."
Nobel Laureate Desmond Tutu

Have you ever *played* with your pain?

I don't mean to offend you with that question. Pain is serious, sometimes deadly serious. We all feel pain, now more than ever after years of pandemic, war, the forced migration of millions, and political conflict tearing at the heart of our homeland. Each morning as we check our newsfeeds, we find more pain. Then, we see that pain transmitted into violence, from abusive words to mass shootings to full-scale wars. We become accustomed to that daily currency of pain flowing around us until things that should shock us—don't anymore.

But did you know there is a distance, however small it may be, between pain and our reaction to pain?

And did you know we can transform pain in many ways, including playing with it?

We can begin that transformation with the stories we tell and share with others: the stories we choose to collect throughout our day—and the stories we choose to pass along to friends and family. This implies a rhythm of talking and listening, and in this process silence is as important as the words we use. If we listen carefully and empathically to those we encounter, we can expand that distance between pain and reaction. In that space, we can "play with"—and perhaps even reshape and redirect—our pain.

This book explores the power we hold in our individual hearts and minds, in our families, in our friendships, and in our spiritual communities to transform pain and discover resilient resources that can *heal us all*. Does that phrase sound too sweeping? Remember, as you read these pages: You are not alone, even in the depths of your pain. Pain is a universal human experience. And for millions of people of faith, like me, God is at the center. Yet even as I write that, I must admit that through the centuries, honest people of faith have not been always sure of where God is, or what God's role is, in the midst of suffering. Elie Wiesel famously wrote about how, in the horrors of Auschwitz, three Jewish scholars put God on trial for the Holocaust.

I have spent a lifetime trying to solve the theological riddle of pain. Perhaps you have as well. As I was finishing this book, I noted the passing of Rabbi Harold Kushner—along with more than four million readers who explored the timeless questions in Kushner's *When Bad Things Happen to Good People*. Regardless of whether you agreed or disagreed with Rabbi Kushner's conclusions, his book struck a powerful chord. My own previous book, *Reading Buechner*, raised similar questions and shared some of the wisdom I have gleaned from the bestselling Christian author Frederick Buechner.

The universal truth is that *everyone*, at some point in life, asks: "Why, God?" Or perhaps you have worded the question: "Why did God allow *this* to happen!?!" Or: "Why did *this* happen to *me*, O God!?"

Those questions are aimed at the contradiction that people have wrestled with down through the millennia between the existence of pain—and God's ultimate power and loving goodness. How can these things both exist? In asking these questions, we stand in a long line of men and women, from ancient Greek philosophers and the central character in the Bible's book of Job—to the authors of the Psalms. The questions don't go away—they are explored by new generations today in movies based on Marvel comic books, graphic novels, and powerful television dramas.

"Why, God?"

The question leaps out at us when we least expect it. Recently, I was driving a rental car a couple of thousand miles away from home. I was about to turn when another car came straight at me, traveling at a high speed. The other driver saw me at the last possible second and screeched to a halt, no more than three inches short of my car.

"Thank you, Jesus!" I cried.

But did Jesus have anything to do with my happy outcome? Why was I spared a head-on collision? Why did that driver stop short when others do not? That same week, I heard a horrible story about a 3-year-old killed by a motorist. Could God have stopped the driver speeding toward me—and let that other driver kill an innocent child?

A few years ago, someone committed a robbery in my town and was being chased in his car by the police down a city street. The robber's car was approaching 100 miles per hour when the driver lost control crossing railroad tracks. His car plowed into an oncoming car driven by a young woman, on the cusp of college and a promising life, killing her. The robber was unharmed. If God is all powerful and all loving, how could something like that happen? "Why, God?"

~

"Theodicy" is the term for the theological attempt to answer the questions created by the existence of evil. "Lament" is a religious response to tragedy, a spiritual practice often neglected in our upbeat, success-oriented churches. At different times in my life, I have been stuck on the theodicy questions when I would have been better off entering deeply into lament. Lament is a beginning step to transforming pain. Telling our story can be the next step.

Throughout his ninety years, Nobel Laureate Desmond Tutu often offered that same prescription. In countless conversations, Tutu would confront the mystery of horrific tragedy by saying: "I cannot solve that puzzle—but let me tell you a story." And then he would tell a true story of trauma, sharing a lament with his listeners, often coupled with a transformation that surprised and inspired. At that point, his listeners had all but forgotten the original puzzle because they were engaged in Tutu's storytelling. How often did Tutu recommend this formula? In the 2014 book he co-authored with his daughter Mpho Tutu, an Anglican priest, called *The Book of Forgiving: The Fourfold Path for Healing Ourselves and Our World*, the Tutus used the word "story" 262 times! After all, the first two steps in their Fourfold Path are: "Telling the Story" and "Naming the Hurt." Those two steps are followed by: "Granting Forgiveness" and "Renewing or Releasing the Relationship."

What the Tutus describe is much like visiting a charred landscape after a forest fire, as the first green shoots of new pines are piercing the layer of ash. If you have ever seen such dewy green shoots reaching toward the sunshine, then you have wordlessly witnessed this process of new life rising from trauma.

Together, as we share stories, we find hope simply through the act of telling our stories together. In the telling and listening, we are affirming that we are not alone. Some stories bolster our faith while others challenge it. Yet even as stories challenge our religious faith, our voices are calling out like the beleaguered father in Mark 9, who cries, "Lord, I believe. Help my unbelief." Just think about this story from Mark 9 for a moment. The father's feelings are compelling, and, more than that, so similar to our feelings we resonate with them 2,000 years later.

In their book, the Tutus write about that transformative power of telling our stories and naming our hurts with others encircling us: "I have my story and they have their story, and together we have our story." It's the same power that Bill W. and Dr. Bob unlocked when they founded the Twelve Step movement that now circles our globe.

Storytelling in a community provides a way into and through things, even things that make no sense. For example, the book of Job doesn't provide a series of rational, propositional answers to the questions raised by the existence of evil. Instead, Job tells a memorable story. When God speaks out of the whirlwind to Job, God tells a story about creation and reminds Job of his place in it. When we voice our stories, we connect with a larger story and find new meaning in our lives.

This book is a compilation of stories of people who summoned resilience and hope in the midst of great suffering by choosing to do something redemptive with their pain. These are stories of people who do not simply transmit their pain—they transform their pain.

This redemptive process has been called "the stewardship of pain," a phrase I learned from the author and pastor Frederick Buechner. As we explore stories together, I'll begin with one that explains how the concept of the stewardship of pain became so meaningful to me.

2

I'll Go First

"My story is important not because it is mine, God knows, but because if I tell it anything like right, the chances are you will recognize that in many ways it is also yours. ... It is precisely through these stories in all their particularity, as I have long believed and often said, that God makes himself known to each of us most powerfully and personally."

Frederick Buechner, from Telling Secrets

In the summer of 1985, I was working as the director of the Christian youth ministry Young Life in Holland, Michigan, taking summer Greek at Western Theological Seminary, and planning a late August wedding with my fiancée, Gretchen. In order to save money, I'd moved out of my apartment and had figured out a schedule of housesitting for a number of friends that would carry me through that summer.

Most of the houses were empty, but one came with Craig, a high school student involved in Young Life, whose parents were away. On a mid-July evening I was wrapping up my time at Craig's house—his parents were due back soon and I was slated to head to another house that weekend. Gretchen had offered to come by after work and make some tacos for dinner and then was going to address wedding invitations, which we were already a little late in mailing. I needed to study Greek vocabulary for a test the next morning.

When Gretchen arrived a few minutes after five, I was drowsing on a family room couch. Craig was lying down across the room on another couch. We had a Chicago Cubs game on and we gave Gretchen some flak for waking us up. She shook her head and left the room.

A few moments later she suffered a massive stroke. She was 24 and, up to that moment, in great health. She called to me from the little bathroom off the kitchen, and something in her voice made me take her seriously.

"Something's happened," she said.

I could see things weren't right. The left side of her face looked like it was melting and there was drool coming out of that side of her mouth. Some tics or spasms were starting on the right side of her face. I asked if she could walk, and she took one step toward me and collapsed. Fortunately, the bathroom was so small she fell toward me.

I caught her and more or less dragged her out to the living room and called to Craig for help. By that point, she'd started going into a grand mal seizure and both her right arm and right leg were moving uncontrollably. The left side of her body was motionless.

Out of nowhere, on an otherwise beautiful Thursday evening, the worst was happening. I go through life with a worried voice in the back of my head that always expects the worst to happen. Now it was.

The hospital was only a couple of blocks away and I figured I could get her to the emergency room before an ambulance would even get to where we were. Craig and I both tried to pick her up at the same time and it was like something out of a Laurel and Hardy movie. I went left when he went right. Craig took charge—which was really helpful because I was losing it.

"I'll pick her up! You open the doors!" he shouted. We got her in the car, and I had her at the hospital within ten minutes of the stroke. These days, there are clot busting drugs that can be administered that can reverse the effects of a stroke. We missed that medical breakthrough by about a decade.

A nurse was coming off duty and saw the frantic way I drove up to the emergency room entryway and grabbed a wheelchair. As we took Gretchen inside, she slumped onto her left side while her right arm and leg swung wildly.

The person at the emergency room desk asked if this was normal behavior for Gretchen, which about caused me to blow my top. Then, in an instant, Gretchen was wheeled into a treatment room, and I was alone in the waiting area.

I wasn't alone for long. The hospital chaplain was a friend, and he was on his way home for the night when he saw me. He stayed and started going back and forth between the treatment room and where I was, relaying information. I'm not sure how long he remained at the hospital—maybe an extra three or four hours. I made one phone call to tell a friend what was happening. That friend showed up within minutes, but not before calling many others. Before long the waiting area filled with a community of concerned people who did the best thing they could do—they showed up.

Even though this happened almost forty years ago, parts of that night are as fresh as if they happened yesterday. I remember the emergency room physician taking me into an office so I could call Gretchen's parents in Colorado. Not only did he give me a phone to use in those pre-cellphone days when calling long distance was a big deal, he stayed and got on the phone with Gretchen's parents to give his diagnosis and answer their questions.

I remember that the first friend I called was still there after midnight. He asked if I was ready to go home and when I said yes he asked when the last time I had eaten was. He took me to an all-night diner. He just wanted to make sure I was okay.

I tried to eat but couldn't.

One other experience that night lingers in my memory in a less-than-encouraging way. I wrote about this in the introduction to my book *Reading Buechner,* and will repeat some of that here, but let me first say something I didn't say in *Reading Buechner.* People who read that earlier version have asked what happened to Gretchen. I was so anxious to get on to the Frederick Buechner part of my book that I skipped right over Gretchen. That was a mistake.

Doctors don't know what caused her stroke. They have theories, but nothing definitive. She was in critical care for over a week and then transferred to a trauma rehab hospital in nearby Grand Rapids. She spent eight weeks there. The other people in the hospital recovering from strokes were in their 70s and 80s. We were married six weeks after her stroke on a weekend pass from the hospital. They let her out on a Friday but I had to take her back Sunday morning. Our big wedding was shaved down to about thirty people—the wedding party and immediate family. We got married sitting down because she couldn't walk. Once out of the hospital, she spent several months in outpatient therapy. It was a year before she could return to work and five years before she could drive again. Despite being labeled "high risk" for pregnancies, she gave birth to a healthy daughter and then a healthy son. She says changing diapers was the best physical therapy she ever did. Although she will never have the full use of her left arm and hand and limps with her left leg, she has recovered amazingly well and lived a full life.

But don't sugarcoat any of this: The stroke has affected her every single day for the past thirty-eight years. Yet as much as we wish it had not happened, it's impossible now to imagine our lives any other way. Living with the consequences of this attack on her well-being has become an integral part of who we are. In some ways, it defines us. In other ways, we refuse to let it define us.

Even though the stroke happened to Gretchen, there is a sense in which it also happened to me. As one of my seminary professors put it, I became a secondary sufferer.

After a while that night in the emergency room, I began to let myself feel what was happening. When trauma happens, our brains are controlled by stress hormones that take our rational thought processes offline and we go into fight, flight, or freeze mode. Once I had gotten Gretchen to the hospital, those hormones began to wear off and I started thinking about what was happening. The immediate question was whether she was going to live or die. I wasn't sure and started imagining life as someone whose fiancée had died. No, I said to myself: We're in the right place, she's getting treatment, she's going to live. Then I started wondering what sort of person she would be following this incident. I suspected from the first moment at Craig's house that she was having a stroke. The doctors confirmed that. I knew it was a brain injury and wondered how much brain damage had occurred. What if she didn't know me anymore? Would the damage be reversible? Would we still get married?

Those questions pushed me down into my chair and I started to cry.

I was sitting between two men who were older and wiser than me. One of them noticed I was crying and put his hand on my shoulder. I thought he was going to say something empathetic. Instead, he said, "Get a hold of yourself. Stop crying. You need to be strong. She needs you to be strong."

I described the aftermath of this in *Reading Buechner*: "In one way he was right. She would need a lot of strength from me, more than I ever imagined I had. But in every other way he was wrong.

The best thing for me would have been to allow myself to feel what was happening. Instead, I did what he said. I pulled myself together. I stopped crying. I stopped feeling. I buried the pain. My friend gave bad advice, but he was simply saying what he thought was the right thing to do in the moment. I'm the one who took it."

~

In the chapters that follow, I not only tell the stories of people who have experienced significant trauma but I also process these stories with a subject matter expert who brings wisdom and insight. I'm going to process this first story with Frederick Buechner. His essay "Adolescence and the Stewardship of Pain" changed my life when I read it a few years after Gretchen's stroke. Although Buechner died in 2022, his powerful words live on.

In the early 1990s, Buechner gave a number of messages at the Laity Lodge in Texas, describing the pain of his complicated and dysfunctional family of origin, culminating in Buechner's father's suicide when Buechner was only 10. One of the stories he told was this: One night when both of his parents had been drinking and arguing, Buechner's mother came into his bedroom—he was 7 or 8 years old at the time—handed him the keys to the family car and told him not to give the keys to his father. A short while later, Buechner's father came into the bedroom and pleaded with his young son to give him the keys. Meanwhile, Buechner's mother came into the room and berated his father for disgracing himself in front of his young son.

Can you imagine being a child in a situation like that?

Five decades later, Buechner read an account of this evening from his book *The Wizard's Tide* at the Laity Lodge. "I could see," he wrote in *The Clown in the Belfry*, "that they were moved by it as I read it not because I had written it with any particular eloquence but because, as best I could, I had written it in the simple language of a child in a way that must have awakened in them similar painful memories of their own childhoods."

Afterwards, Laity Lodge Director Howard Butt approached Buechner and said, "You have had a good deal of pain in your life, and you have been a good steward of it."

Butt's comment opened a new idea and led Buechner to reframe the concept of stewardship in the essay "Adolescence and the Stewardship of Pain." Buechner interprets one of Jesus' memorable stories, the parable of the talents in Matthew 25, to be about pain. In that story, a man goes on a journey and gives his servants different amounts of his wealth (called "talents") to manage. Two servants somehow trade and invest the talents they are given so they are doubled when the master returns. The third servant gives in to his fear and buries his talent in the ground so it will be safe when the master returns. On that day, things don't go well for the play-it-safe servant. After praising the first two with the words "Well done, good and faithful servant, enter into the joy of your master," the master explodes with rage at the third servant and banishes him to the outer darkness, where there is weeping and gnashing of teeth.

This is an amazing story for Jesus to tell. An old neighbor of mine, a lifelong church member named Stan, who was in his 80s, sheepishly admitted to me that he struggled mightily with this parable. Stan worried that he might be committing blasphemy by saying this, but he couldn't understand why the guy who played it safe was treated so harshly.

One way ministers deal with the incongruity of the parable is by saying it's about managing money. It feels like I've heard a thousand similar sermons on this parable that some way or another all say we're supposed to do something positive with the financial resources we're given for the sake of the kingdom of God. The parable tends to be revisited on "Stewardship Sunday," when ministers (often with some embarrassed awkwardness) encourage their parishioners to dig deep in their pockets and give to the church.

Buechner reframes the parable by asking: What if the pain we experience is something entrusted to us—something we are to be good stewards of?

Because pain overwhelms us emotionally, the typical survival response to pain is to bury it, akin to the play-it-safe servant in Jesus' parable. Buechner writes, "'Wicked and slothful' is what the rich man calls the third servant, who in so many ways can stand for us all—wicked in burying what he should have held to the light and made something of; slothful because playing it safe is another way of not really playing it at all."

We bury our pain in multiple ways: in our busyness, our addictions, our compulsions, and our consumption. Burying pain is a survival strategy. But it is not a way to thrive or grow.

What does it mean to follow the example of the first two servants in Jesus' story and somehow do something with our pain, instead of burying it? What does it look like to live out of our pain, enabling us to relate to others on the deepest levels?

"Being a good steward of your pain," Buechner writes, "involves ... being alive to your life. It involves taking the risk of being open, of reaching out, of keeping in touch with the pain ... because at no time more than at a painful time do we live out of the depths of who we are instead of out of the shallows."

Buechner says there is no guarantee we will find a pearl in those depths, or find a happy end to our pain, or even any end at all. But we have a chance of discovering, in those depths, who we truly are and of discovering we are not alone in our pain.

Our culture doesn't call us to these depths. I received a direct mail advertising piece the other day with this headline: "Imagine A Life Without Pain. It's Possible!" That's an illusion. Life is never that simple or tidy. Regardless of the advertiser's pitch, to be human is to experience pain, both physical pain and emotional pain. We fool ourselves if we think we can avoid pain or just endure it and get on with our lives.

I struggled to feel any emotions in the aftermath of Gretchen's stroke. I simply felt numb. In some ways, this is a reflection of the way men are socialized in our culture. Although there is evidence this is changing in some circles, I was told big boys don't cry. If you got hurt in a game of football or baseball, you got up and carried on. Woe to the crybaby who let out tears. And if your heart was broken, you had permission to feel anger, but not much else.

When my friend told me to pull myself together that night in the hospital waiting room, he was following a script well-known to men of my generation. It's about being stoic, having a stiff upper lip, and projecting strength. As Buechner says, that's a way to survive the immediate trauma, but not a way to live and not a way to grow.

Buechner's essay invited me to something different. I felt him asking what sort of steward I was going to be of the horrible pain of Gretchen's stroke. I had tried burying it and knew that didn't work. Could I do something redemptive with it instead?

When I read that essay by Buechner, I cried for the first time since my friend in the emergency room told me to pull myself together. I couldn't have stopped crying if I'd wanted to, and I didn't want to. I just let it come. I remember wondering: How did Frederick Buechner, a writer and pastor who lived in Vermont, know so much about me?

Over the years, I have found something redemptive in simply sharing both this story and Buechner's call to be a good steward of pain. Every time I tell this story, I feel great resonance with those listening. People often respond by telling me their stories, often stories about being a secondary sufferer with a sick spouse or child. The stories are heartbreaking, yet I don't feel depressed when I hear them—I feel hopeful because I sense healing is happening in the act of sharing the story.

The people you will meet in the following pages have experienced extraordinary pain and suffering and somehow not only taken that pain into their lives but blessed others through it. They've been good stewards of their pain.

I've often wondered, "How do they go on?"

These pages offer their stories as explanation. As I mentioned, in addition to telling their stories, I process each story with someone who has done a lot of thinking about the particular pain being explored. The reflections on each story provide a commentary to help you go deeper.

The stories reflect my four-decade ministry career, which has been spent with Young Life, Western Theological Seminary, and the Reformed Church in America. Almost everyone in the book is connected to me through one of those organizations. The people interviewed run their stories through their particular religious lenses, seeking to understand what the stories say about God and our place in the world. As I've worked on this, a few people have commented, "Gee, you know a lot of people who have gone through traumatic experiences."

That's not true. I know as many as you do. There's a lot of pain in the world. If we open our eyes, it's everywhere. But we often look away, not having the will to engage with what's right in front of us.

By opening yourself to these stories, may you find healing and hope.

3

Murder Mysteries

"I'm not an evil man."
Clarence Hayes, before he pulled the trigger

"Hope is for all of us, even Clarence Hayes."
Psychologist Daniel Rooks

Ron Nelson made an unexpected career move. After years of climbing the academic career ladder, moving his wife, Marian, and their two sons from college town to college town and piling up advanced degrees, he had made it in academia, securing tenure at Michigan State University. This was the dream: tenure at a major university.

But after a decade in East Lansing, a few things unsettled him. He taught introductory humanities courses in massive auditoriums filled with as many as four hundred students. Because of the size of the courses, his students were anonymous. And there was his Christian faith. Raised in the very conservative Plymouth

Brethren church, he'd found a larger intellectual framework for his faith in the Reformed Church in America (RCA) while doing his Ph.D. at the University of Michigan. But now, at Michigan State, he didn't see a clear way to integrate his faith with his teaching. He felt there wasn't enough room in a public university to explore the many questions at the intersection of faith and learning he wanted to entertain.

Then, there was his teenaged son Roger. The Nelsons lived outside East Lansing in suburban Okemos, and Ron and Marian were concerned about Roger. Although very bright, he was not excelling academically. Instead, he seemed focused solely on sports, girls, and popularity. Years later, Roger would discover that he had an undiagnosed learning disability which made schoolwork difficult. At the time, his parents thought: Maybe their son would straighten out eventually, but they wondered if Okemos was the right place for him. The trajectory of Roger's life didn't feel promising.

Ron worked out a deal to spend a sabbatical year at tiny Northwestern College in remote Orange City, Iowa. He wanted to try teaching at a private Christian college with Christian colleagues. His classes would only have twenty students, and Ron would also have opportunities to interact with his students in several ways outside the classroom. Northwestern was affiliated with the RCA and filled with students and faculty sincere about the Christian faith. On top of that, Roger, a sophomore in high school, would be thrust into a much different environment in a small town where Iowa meets Nebraska, South Dakota, and Minnesota.

That year turned into the rest of Ron Nelson's academic career. Instead of returning to Michigan State, he took more than a fifty percent pay cut and traded his earlier academic ideal for contentment.

For Roger there was no fast-track party crowd to hang out with in Orange City. After high school, with lots of parental input, he enrolled at Calvin College in Grand Rapids, Michigan, a premier Christian liberal arts school in the Reformed tradition. Unfortunately, any progress Roger had made during his last couple of years in Orange City regressed at Calvin. Roger didn't make it past his sophomore year. He had seen the new movie *Animal House* and felt the lifestyle of the members of the Delta House was the ideal. As a result, Roger was a consistent visitor to the dean's office, in trouble for pranks, drinking, poor academics, and what he now calls "general knuckleheadedness." The dean flatly told Roger to work on his identity crisis at some other school.

Roger returned to Orange City and enrolled at Northwestern, where his father was a member of the history faculty. Slowly, Roger began to mature. He did Northwestern's Chicago metro semester and worked at Roseland Christian Ministries, a Reformed ministry among the poor on the city's south side. Roger found a mentor in Tony Van Zanten, Roseland's pastor, and for the first time felt a sense of call and purpose in his life. He felt similar things when he started spending summers at CranHill Ranch, an RCA camp in Michigan, working as a counselor. Then, as college was winding down, he spent four months in Hong Kong, working in a camp for Vietnamese refugees. As he returned from Hong Kong, Roger felt convinced he was supposed to work alongside poor people but knew he didn't need to go halfway around the world to find that— there was plenty of need at Roseland. At times he'd dreamed of becoming a lawyer who fought for justice in the inner city, but his mediocre grades closed those doors. He wanted to make a difference in the city, like Pastor Tony. Roger could see himself doing what Pastor Tony did, and since a couple of his good friends had enrolled at Western Theological Seminary, an RCA school in Holland, Michigan, Roger followed suit.

After a lackluster initial year at Western, Roger returned to Chicago and Roseland as part of SCUPE, the Seminary Consortium for Urban Pastoral Education. Once again, he felt in his element, although the academic dimensions of SCUPE were a slog. He spent the year as the live-in manager of a shelter for homeless men in Roseland. The following summer he went back to CranHill as the program director, and met a young woman named Sandi, who was destined to be his wife. After the year with SCUPE, he returned to seminary in Michigan, and before long Roger and Sandi were engaged. Ron and Marian Nelson wanted to get to know their future daughter-in-law, so they arranged a spring weekend together in Chicago.

As the weekend closed, the four of them worshipped together at Roseland. It was March 17, 1985, a sunny St. Patrick's Day, and the city was coming alive after a long winter. Roger played guitar and led the singing at church. At one point during the service, one of the congregants testified about his progress overcoming addiction and Ron Nelson made his hands into fists, which he shook triumphantly in the air, like an athletic coach, as a sign of encouragement. Ron was obviously moved by the celebratory and rich worship service, and one can only imagine Ron's thoughts as he watched his son Roger lead music. Roger had come so far. Although a seminarian, he was already doing ministry in a place of genuine need, and he was engaged to a wonderful young woman. The trajectory of Roger's life looked far different than it had a few years earlier. Ron's career move may have cost him academic status and financial reward, but this was far better.

As the service ended, Ron told Pastor Tony, "Thanks for letting us be here, I feel so refreshed." Then the Nelsons went into the parking lot and stood talking while they discussed where they would go for lunch. After their lunch, Ron and Marian were going to head back to Iowa, while Roger and Sandi were bound for Michigan.

∼

That same morning, Clarence Hayes had a gun and a need for money to supply his drug addiction. He'd been foiled by bullet-proof glass when he tried to rob a liquor store two blocks away from Roseland about the time the worship service was ending. Then, as he walked down the alley alongside the church, he saw opportunity in the form of the Nelson family. He went into the parking lot, confronted the Nelsons, and ordered them into Ron's and Marian's car. Ron took the driver's seat with Marian next to him and Roger and Sandi sat in the back. Hayes kept the driver's door open and crouched behind it, next to Ron Nelson, sticking his gun into Ron's side, as he went through their wallets and purses.

"Somebody's going to get killed if you hold out on me," Hayes said.

Roger leaned forward and did most of the talking, assuring Hayes that they weren't holding anything back. Roger had been robbed once before in Chicago by someone who held a knife to his throat to steal a five-pound block of government cheese Roger was holding. This felt like that, something he just had to get through. He wondered how he was going to make getting robbed "all right" with his mom and dad and Sandi's parents. As Roger asserted that they'd given Hayes everything, Hayes became agitated and moved his gun to Roger's neck, telling him to shut up. Hayes saw a check-book in Ron's pocket, but Ron insisted the checkbook would be of no use to Hayes.

"I'm not an evil man," Hayes said and moved the gun away from Roger—back toward Ron. Donna Van Zanten, Pastor Tony's wife, saw the Nelsons still in the parking lot and went to check on them with her son Kent, a high school football player. Hayes ordered them into the backseat of the car alongside Roger and Sandi. Finally, after several minutes, Hayes seemed satisfied. At the moment it looked like the ordeal was over, Hayes, without provocation, fired the gun into the side of Ron Nelson, who slumped into Marian's lap.

Roger frantically climbed over Kent Van Zanten to get out of the car and run for help. As he raced across the parking lot, he actually ran side-by-side for a few moments to the entrance of the parking lot with Hayes. Hayes then turned back into the alley and Roger turned the other direction and went into the church, telling Pastor Tony what had happened and picking up an in-house intercom phone in a futile attempt to call for help.

"It took me twenty-five years," Roger said, "to realize I should have climbed into the driver's seat and taken my dad to the hospital, which was only a couple of blocks away." Roseland Christian Ministries is at the intersection of 109th and Michigan Avenue. Roseland Community Hospital is two blocks south, just around the corner on 111th Street.

However, after the emergency call was placed from inside the church, Roger got back outside to find an ambulance crew tending to Ron—but the ambulance didn't speed away immediately. Ron Nelson was already dead.

Nevertheless, they transported Ron to the hospital, where a nurse said, "We're unable to resuscitate him," which initially didn't sound to Roger like it meant his father was dead.

In the small room where the family and members of the Roseland community had gathered, Marian kept saying, "Everything will be okay if he's alive." Finally, they were told Ron was dead.

Roger walked out of the room, slapped his hand against the wall, and shouted, "They killed my father!" To this day he isn't sure what or who he meant by "they," although an African American nurse took it as a broad racial indictment. This story has a racial component. The Nelsons and Van Zantens are white. Clarence Hayes and most of the Roseland Congregation are Black.

The nurse said, "We're sorry, but it wasn't all of us."

One of the members of the Roseland congregation, also African American, put her arm around Roger and said, "Don't you worry about him. This is my son."

~

Roger and Sandi spent the afternoon in a nearby police station, looking at mug shots. Meanwhile, officers at the scene soon learned the shooter's identity. There were plenty of people outside that beautiful spring day who had seen Hayes in the alley. Hayes was arrested a few weeks later and Roger and Sandi, along with the Van Zantens, were asked to pick the shooter out of a lineup.

"It was like something out of a cop show," Roger said. "Driving from Michigan I wondered if I would recognize him, since it had been a few weeks. The moment I saw him I knew it was him."

In separate lineups, Roger, Sandi, and both Van Zantens immediately identified Hayes as the gunman. An unexpected emotion hit Roger in the police station. "It was the first time I felt fear. There was Clarence Hayes, a few feet away from me, and I was afraid. I just kept thinking about how many guns were in the building and I knew not everything that happens in police stations is good. It filled me with fear."

It was Hayes' fourth felony arrest. In an earlier robbery, he'd used a similar tactic, that time pressing a screwdriver into the neck of a woman while crouching alongside the open driver's door of her car.

~

Ron Nelson's funeral was held in Orange City. A group of Roger's seminary friends attended. That night, Jerry Sittser, who was the chaplain at Northwestern, hosted Roger and his friends for dinner. (Six years later, Sittser would be visited by unspeakable tragedy when a drunk driver would cross over the median at high speed and crash into the minivan Sittser was driving. Sittser's wife, mother, and 4-year-old daughter were killed. Sittser would write his story in *A Grace Disguised*.)

"I remember sitting at Jerry Sittser's house the night of the funeral eating spaghetti," Roger said. "I just started crying. Everyone stopped eating and waited. They just sat and let it be okay. I had a sense that this is what care and community looks like. I pulled myself together and we went on eating."

Roger felt awkward returning to seminary. He'd often sit in class feeling dazed, with tears in his eyes. He does recall being helped by two of his professors. One, who had recently lost a son to suicide, simply moved toward Roger empathically. The professor's own loss was too recent and he couldn't find words to speak, but Roger felt the comfort of his caring presence, and felt this man knew what Roger was feeling. The second professor had slowly and agonizingly lost a 20-year-old son to cancer a few years earlier. That professor stopped Roger in the hall to express his sympathy, and then told Roger that at the time of his son's death, he thought that even if God himself were to appear and write down the reasons for the professor's son's death on a piece of paper, he would crumple the paper and throw it back in God's face, because no explanation could make what happened seem right.

Tom Stark, the pastor of University Reformed Church in East Lansing, where the Nelsons had once worshipped, drove across the state to visit Roger. "We walked along the pier at Lake Michigan," Roger said. "I don't remember what we talked about; I just remember that he cared. He was present and made the effort to see me. I thought, 'This is what it means to be a pastor,' and knew it was what I wanted to do."

~

Clarence Hayes' trial was held more than a year after his arrest. Roger and Sandi, who were now married, were witnesses, along with the Van Zantens. Marian Nelson was spared the trauma of testifying. Hayes' defense was that this was a case of mistaken identity. He claimed he'd been home at the time, watching a March Madness NCAA basketball game on television, although the game he said he'd been watching did not take place the day of the murder.

Against his attorney's counsel, Hayes took the stand in his own defense. "I feel bad for the Nelsons," he said, "but I don't understand why they would lie about me. I'm not an evil man."

Roger felt anger surge when he heard Hayes say, "I'm not an evil man," the same line he'd said while jamming his gun into Ron Nelson's side. "I'd felt an overwhelming sadness before that," Roger said. "Sadness about the knot of poverty, addiction, gun violence, racism, inadequate health care, and the whole system that nobody knows how to untangle that we were all a part of. But 'I'm not an evil man' made me angry. Why couldn't he just tell the truth?"

Hayes was found guilty of murder and six counts of armed robbery. There was much speculation whether the judge would give Hayes the death penalty. At the sentencing, the judge noted the crime showed a blatant disregard for life and was committed on the grounds of a church. The judge also said he felt an affinity with Roger, and then sentenced Clarence Hayes to death. The courtroom was packed, with Hayes' family on one side and the Nelsons and Van Zantens and various court officials on the other.

Roger felt similar to how he'd felt earlier at the police station, like he was out of body, watching himself in a television show, and when the sentence was announced the room erupted. Roger, meanwhile, felt lost and alone, as the drama unfolded in front of him.

An appeal was filed, citing, among other things, the words the judge had said about feeling an affinity with Roger as evidence of prejudice against Hayes. The death penalty was overturned by the appeal and the sentence was changed to life in prison without parole. Once again, Roger had to appear in court, this time to read a statement about the impact of the crime on his family. Each court appearance ripped open the wound and revisited the pain of Ron Nelson's murder. The Nelsons did not advocate for the death penalty, they simply wanted assurance that Clarence Hayes would never be free to do to another family what he had done to theirs. Hayes remains in prison, and the Nelson family has not had contact with him since the appeal.

Occasionally, though, reminders surface. For example, when Roger and Sandi's daughter was a teenager, she and a young man who sat next to her in a high school class figured out who each other was: she was Roger and Sandi's daughter and the granddaughter of Ron Nelson; her classmate was the nephew of Clarence Hayes.

Marian Nelson moved from Iowa to Michigan to be closer to Roger and his brother and their families. In some ways she moved on, making friends, getting a job, becoming part of a widow's support group, joining a church, and seeing men socially. But she grieved the loss of her husband and missed him daily. She often steered the conversation to Ron at family gatherings, something Roger resisted because it was so painful. Marian Nelson died of natural causes on Thanksgiving Day, 2019.

Roger graduated from seminary and kept moving forward in ministry. He didn't know what else to do. He felt the sadness of grief and sought to knit the pain he'd experienced into his being without "making it a commodity." Roseland remained the place that felt like his spiritual home, the only place he felt a sense of call. After seminary he returned to Chicago, working in the city with Young Life. After a while he moved and taught religion at Christian high schools, first in Grand Rapids and then in the Chicago suburbs. Later, he took a call to Schenectady, New York, and joined the staff of a large Reformed church.

One of his friends in Schenectady was a therapist, and they started working together, fifteen years after the murder. "We didn't

focus on the trauma as much as we sorted out my relationship
with my dad," Roger said. "I remember talking through things like
if I had my dad's blessing." That friendship, with occasional therapeutic conversations, continues.

For the past twenty years, Roger has been the pastor of Hope
Christian Reformed Church in Oak Forest, Illinois. His congregation partners with Roseland Christian Ministries, and it's not
unusual for Roger to visit the site of his dad's murder multiple
times in a week. Sandi now works at Roseland, and, up until his
death a short while ago, regularly interacted with Clarence Hayes'
brother.

"From the beginning," Roger said, "I felt like I had stepped into
the pool of gun violence. It's a big, big pool."

How big? According to the Chicago police, there were almost
400 people killed by gun violence in Chicago that year. According
to the *Chicago Tribune* there were 900. "Many people," Roger said,
"think the actual number is around 700. There's such a deep sadness that pervades the whole incident. Clarence Hayes has become
emblematic of all that stuff to me. I tend to think of him that way
rather than as an actual person. I have tended to think of him as an
eruption of the brokenness of creation. I look at my life now and
sometimes ask myself if what I've experienced has made me better
at what I do, made me a better pastor. It probably has. But I would
trade that in a heartbeat to have my dad back."

As Roger and I talked, almost four decades after his father's
murder, Roger was surprised that he started crying.

"I just haven't gone through this from beginning to end in a
while," he said, "but that's grief for you. I often say grief is jagged.
Life goes on, eventually you live and laugh and love again, but then
something will happen and you get snagged. You're never done
with it. I remember thinking I could never watch TV or a movie
again. There were all those cop shows and I would ask, 'Why do
we watch this for entertainment?' But then Sandi and I went to

the movies to see *The Color Purple* when it came out at Christmas a few months after Dad's murder, and towards the end there's a scene where the two sisters are reunited and they run toward each other across a field of purple flowers. I was absolutely shattered … because I saw my mom and dad being reunited."

Roger said, "The only thing that makes any sense to me, or gives me any hope, is the notion that creation ends like that. I hope that somehow, some way, all of it—including Clarence Hayes, and his parents, and his son—that somehow, to echo Julian of Norwich, it will all be made well and all manner of things will be well."

Roger's story is both devastatingly sad and hopeful. He's a great minister, but also someone tied deeply into the lives of the members of his congregation. How could Roger not get stuck in the trauma of this story? How could he become such a good pastor and such a great preacher? How could he become such a good steward of his pain?

~

I turned to Dr. Daniel Rooks for help understanding Roger's story.

I chose Dan Rooks for a couple of reasons. Dan is a psychologist in private practice who has helped a lot of people, and I knew he'd bring insight and wisdom to the story. But Dan also has spent significant time working with prison inmates, and since the criminal justice system figures prominently in this story, I thought he may offer thoughts about that part of the story as well.

Sure enough, the first thing Dan said to me was, "You only have half of the story."

Dan immediately focused on the story in its largest sense: "Two people who did not know each other have a brief encounter that changes both of their lives forever. One came out of an alley, the

other out of a church. Those are both factual and symbolic loca-
tions. They meet each other in a church parking lot, there is a
violent episode—a murder—and then they're both running parallel with each other. What a powerful image! Their paths diverged
as Clarence Hayes went back into the alley and Roger went back
into the church. At certain points the story preceding the murder focused on the trajectory of Roger's life. Roger found himself
by embracing the church and had good mentors and role models
around him. What sort of role models did Clarence Hayes have?
What opportunities did he have—or not have—along the way
that resulted in him being in that alley? What can we say about
the trajectory of his life?"

Dan also made it clear that he entered Roger's story cautiously.
"Roger's story is personal and intimate. It's sacred. I don't know
Roger, but after reading his story I have a great deal of respect for
him. As the judge said, 'I feel an affinity toward him.'"

With these disclaimers in place, Dan and I discussed Roger's
story. Dan believes strongly in the power of story and told me of a
fellow therapist visiting him when he moved into a new office and
saying, "These walls don't have stories yet." The space was furnished
yet incomplete because it had yet to be populated by anyone's story.
Stories are gifts, and without stories our lives are as unfinished as
that office space.

Roger had been surprised by the emotion he felt as he retold
the story to me, and I felt that emotion most intensely when Roger
expressed his frustration at not figuring out for twenty-five years
that he should have just driven his father to the hospital instead
of running for help. I wouldn't call what Roger expressed guilt as
much as disappointment. I understand his disappointment, but
when we talked, I told Roger to let himself off the hook. A lot was
happening in those moments.

I asked Dan to help me understand what happens to our
brains during trauma. He told me that there are stress hormones

like cortisol and adrenaline flowing through our bodies during trauma, which mobilize us for fight or flight. This happens involuntarily—the stress hormones knock logically weighing options offline. Moments before Clarence Hayes shot Ron Nelson, Roger's brain was operating at a rational level, as he thought about how he was going to make the robbery "all right" to his parents and future in-laws. But when the gun was fired, Roger's body mobilized into fight or flight mode and his body—led by his nervous system instead of his brain—reacted. There's simply no way he would have been able to calmly figure out the best option.

There are other points in the story where strong emotions surfaced for Roger. He felt fear in the police station when he was in close proximity to Clarence Hayes, and anger in the courtroom when Hayes said, "I'm not an evil man," the same words he'd said while threatening Ron Nelson with a gun.

"The very emotions Roger identifies—fear and anger—are what Bryan Stevenson, the author of *Just Mercy* and founder of the Equal Justice Initiative, identifies as the basis of much of our justice system," Dan told me. "If we base justice solely on fear and anger, we're basing it on reactions from our nervous systems that don't represent our full capacities. We have to find a way to breathe and slow down enough for those higher systems to come back online."

We tend to imagine the legal system is going to offer healing through the pronouncement of a verdict, but in many cases, it does not do that. According to Dan, the criminal justice side of this story points out both adequacies and inadequacies in our system, which can aggravate trauma as much as alleviate it. One positive example: Roger's mother was spared what Roger experienced during the long process, the constant reopening of the wounds throughout the legal process. That was one way the legal system recognized that this would not be a place for her to find healing, which needed to be a priority for her.

Dan said he wondered about the motivations behind the judge's death sentence. "By saying he felt an affinity with Roger, it's almost as if he was saying, 'I'm going to do this for you. I am going to have this person killed for you.' The judge cited the blatant disregard for life, but what regard was there for Clarence Hayes' life? The courtroom had two sides. One side was Black, filled with the relatives of Clarence Hayes. The other side was white, with the Nelsons and Van Zantens and court officials. When the sentence was announced the Black side erupted in emotion as they felt the disregard for the life of their family member. For them it was one more example of how the system treats people of color. Clarence Hayes was poor, Black, and guilty. His life didn't have value. But the fact that the death penalty was overturned on appeal says something positive about our system. Our system adjusted. However, you'll notice there was no healing or restoration in the legal process for Roger."

Dan quoted Bryan Stevenson again, when it comes to the death penalty, "It's not whether or not someone deserves to die, but if we deserve to kill." Dan said, "In my mind, it's very much like Jesus with the woman caught in adultery in John 8. Jesus didn't advocate for her innocence; he simply pointed out no one had the right to throw the first stone."

I asked Dan about Roger's out of body feelings at the police station and during the trial and he explained two additional concepts connected to trauma: "derealization" and "depersonalization." Derealization is the mental state of feeling detached from one's surroundings, the feeling that things just are not real. Depersonalization is the persistent sense of observing oneself from outside of one's body. These are normal ways our bodies and brains help us deal with trauma, but they can turn into problems if they continue. Dan said it was not surprising Roger would feel that way in court, where he could not access a fight or flight option. He was stuck in that place. Our bodies and brains protect us in those moments by shutting down and disconnecting us from our pain. The nervous system takes over. It's also not surprising Roger felt the same way when he returned to seminary—he was stuck in that place, too, and his reality and the reality of others in that community were highly discordant. You can feel very alone when your experience is starkly out of sync with the people around you.

"You'll notice too," Dan said, "a difference in how Roger experienced grief and how his mother experienced grief. She wanted to talk about Ron but that was too painful for Roger. Talking about Ron gave her something she sought that Roger didn't need. People grieve in different ways. Roger says grief is jagged. I don't know that all grief is jagged, but traumatic grief certainly is jagged. It reflects the jagged nature of trauma. Not all grief is the same."

∾

Although Dan doesn't know Roger, I've known Roger since 1982, when we were seminary students together. I well remember where I was on St. Patrick's Day in 1985 when I learned of Ron Nelson's murder. I was not in the group of seminarians who traveled to Iowa for the funeral only because my aunt and uncle died in a car accident on March 18, the day after Ron Nelson was killed, and I was attending their funeral. Roger remains a dear friend, and I know that fear and anger are not the emotions that rule his life. I also know he was attuned to racial justice issues long before most of our white seminary classmates. His outburst, "They killed my father," was unlike him.

"In spite of all of Roger's experiences and values," Dan said, "he fell into racial blaming for a moment. Racial blaming comes from the fight or flight side of our nervous system and is an expression of fear and anger. It's interesting: Roger exploded and then the nurse had her response. She was offended but kept her cool, said she was sorry about what happened, and then pointed out that 'it wasn't all of us.' My hunch is this was meant educationally, but the real power in that moment came from the Roseland church member who put her arm around Roger and said, 'Don't worry about him. This is my son.' What gets us past interpersonal racial divides? I'm speaking interpersonally here; I know that there are systemic issues as well. But interpersonally, most of us choose the educational approach that the nurse took, thinking that if we just show someone how wrong they are it will make a difference. The problem with that approach is that it can come off as moralistic and get tied up with blame and shame. That's not what changes people's hearts. What really makes a difference is a relationship. Knowing someone. Putting your arm around someone. Again, Roger's trajectory comes up. It was brief, but he could have reduced the world into us or them, Black or white, and gotten stuck there. He came out of it, and I suspect the actual physicality of the woman's touch and embrace allowed his nervous system to shift and brought him back to himself. The nervous system had led the way and taken his conscious values offline. The woman's touch impacted his nervous system and brought him back to himself."

That moment is a deeply powerful moment in a story filled with powerful moments. Dan noted Ron Nelson's enjoyment and identification with hearing a testimony from someone overcoming addiction moments before losing his life to someone whose addiction was out of control. "And then," Dan said, "there's Roger's ability to return frequently to the site of the murder. How can he do that?" Dan felt that Roger's ability to hold the story as part of something bigger had significantly helped him. If Roger had become stuck in the story, the story may have diminished him. By seeing it in the larger context of gun violence, poverty, racial inequality, and other things, the horrendousness of the act is not minimized, but placed in a larger context. "Roger entered this larger context when he felt called to Roseland. This wasn't something he chose. The

Holy Spirit put it on his heart, and Roger knew, as his parents and Sandi and the Van Zantens also knew, that this ministry comes with risks. Going back there after the worst that could happen actually happened gives testimony to the larger context. And Roger mentions it again in the end, when he articulates the sense of hope he had when he saw *The Color Purple* and that beautiful scene of the two women running toward each other. He saw them as his mother and father, and surely hope is there for Ron and Marian Nelson, but it's not just for them. It's for the whole created order. Hope is for all of us, even Clarence Hayes, as Roger says."

~

Roger says that from the beginning that he knew he had just stepped into the large pool of gun violence. For Dan, it's significant that Roger also found himself in the even larger pool of suffering humanity and was met there by others he was already in community with.

"They came forward and met him even more intimately because of this shared knowledge of pain and loss," Dan said. "The fact that decades later Roger can recall the empathetic power of his seminary professors, even one who couldn't find words to speak, and the presence of Tom Stark, and his fellow students eating spaghetti at Jerry Sittser's house, shows the significance of these moments. I'm sure there were dozens if not hundreds of other expressions of empathy. Roger experienced deep connection and compassion with those who preceded him in the knowledge of pain and with those who would follow him in this knowing—those who would find themselves drawn together in a knowledge of pain and the desire to help one another steward that pain together.

"The people who expressed empathy to Roger saved him. I know that's a strong word. They saved him from where the pain may have taken him otherwise. This level of pain and suffering has a way of jarring our system and we run the risk of disconnecting from our humanity, from who we really are. When someone else steps into our pain and suffering, when they aren't afraid and come into it with care, that's huge. What we say matters, I don't want to discount that, but care is less about saying the right thing and more about just showing up. Like the moment with the seminary professor who couldn't speak shows, you don't have to have the right words, or any words at all, you just have to come alongside."

As Dan reflected on the concept of the stewardship of pain, he said that those engaged in stewarding their own pain often discover a particular generativity in relationship to others going through pain. Choosing to turn toward and face one's pain leaves us less afraid of pain and capable of being drawn empathically toward others in the heart of their particular pain. The stewardship of pain cannot occur alone or in isolation. It requires community and relationship.

"I appreciate Roger's honesty," Dan said, "when he admitted that although this experience may have made him a better pastor, there is no way that makes what happened all right. I agree. But it is interesting to note how what happened led Roger into deeper levels of being. It's almost like a Flannery O'Connor story where violence is inextricably entwined with spiritual revelation."

"There's also much we can learn from Ron Nelson," Dan said. "He was a teacher, and we can still learn from him. Success is not merely or meaningfully defined by salary and prestige of position. These achievements, while widely recognized and honored as such by most people, can leave one feeling empty and incomplete. Rather, finding a place in which he could more fully engage his faith and have fewer but deeper relationships with colleagues and students—these things are worth making significant and counter-cultural salary and position sacrifices for."

Dan likes to illustrate this process of growth through pain and suffering by talking about lodgepole pines, which are prolific seed producers. However, those seeds are locked inside of pinecones for years, sometimes fifteen years or more, until a forest fire releases them. Many teachers over the years have used the image of fire releasing lodgepole pine seeds as a metaphor. Dan noted parallels in the significance of religious education, which instills values in the heart so that when the heart breaks there will be something released, which often comes as a surprising discovery.

Throughout Roger's life—the life he'd lived with his parents and in his faith community—things were put into his heart so that when he went through this experience, he was able to hold the trauma without allowing it to degrade or destroy him. A crisis like this reveals character as much as creates character. We discover who we really are by the choices we make in response to our circumstances; we discover our identity as our story unfolds.

As Nazi concentration camp survivor Viktor Frankl said, "Between stimulus and response there is a space. In that space is our power to choose our response. In our response lies our growth and our freedom." Frankl also said that there is one thing that can never be taken away—to choose one's attitude in any set of circumstances.

"I think this is what Roger is referring to," Dan said, "when he said he's taken this experience into his being without letting it become a commodity—which is such an interesting statement. I think he's referring to the power to choose how to respond. Yes, it is true, that in the actual moment of trauma the brain goes offline and we involuntarily react. But that's only in that moment. We still have a tremendous amount of agency.

"Identity is also a recurring theme in this story. Clarence Hayes says it's a case of mistaken identity. Roger is told by the dean at Calvin College to work on his identity crisis someplace else. Roger sees *Animal House* and thinks that's supposed to be his identity.

Finally, at Roseland and CranHill he begins to discover the truest version of himself. Our hyper-Westernized sense of identity is an individualized autonomous self. But that's just not reality. 'Who am I?' isn't the question. 'Whose am I?' is the question. To whom do we belong? What community do we belong to? As we see in this story, mentors and role models along the way make a big impact as we sort this out."

In the end, Dan told me: "My prayer for any of us is that we live in communities that allow us to open our hearts to love fully and suffer well. I believe Roger Nelson has done that. For Roger to open his heart to anyone after an event like this, it was incumbent on him to suffer well. We don't do that alone. We only do that in community with other people. One last observation: People came around him and helped him through this horrific time. As a result, Roger has spent the past several decades in ministry doing that for other people."

Roger Nelson is the pastor of Hope Christian Reformed Church in Oak Forest, Illinois. www.Hope-CRC.org

Daniel Rooks is a clinical psychologist in private practice in Holland, Michigan. He also is widely known for his work with prisoners both in leading classes on nonviolent communication and in advocacy for incarcerated individuals and their families.

4

Quiniece's Legacy

"It's very difficult to find the line between being generous, welcoming, accepting, and forgiving on the one hand, and acknowledging profound injustice on the other. ... Quiniece's story brings up so many factors around it: litigiousness, greed, the unforgiving nature of institutions—all those aspects need to be named. Her story shouldn't just go underground. ... A story like Quiniece's deserves to have a spotlight shown on it."

Marilyn McEntyre

"The number one thing I have learned from this is to take time to slow down and love those in my circle. That's Quiniece's legacy."

Quentin Henry, Quiniece's father

There's something special about Quentin Henry. Call it charisma, electricity, charm, or presence, Quentin has the sort of personality that makes those he's just met not only believe they are friends but feel as if they have been good friends for a long time. He has an easy extroversion and an infectious smile. I have known Quentin for many years, since I was leading a team that hired him to be the co-director for Young Life's ministry in the city of Grand Rapids. Young Life is a nondenominational Christian youth ministry, and I spent the first twenty-nine years of my career working for Young Life.

In almost no time, Quentin and his co-director Fred Comer had recruited several volunteers and established a significant outreach to high school-aged young people in the city schools of Grand Rapids. Most of those young people were Black or Latino. Young Life was founded in Texas in the 1940s and had traditionally been focused on middle class white youth. Our ministry in Grand Rapids did not have a strong track record with young people of color. That began to change under Quentin and Fred's leadership.

I learned much from Quentin about the challenges he faced as a Black man raising a family in our community. I remember riding with him in his van once because I needed to rent some tables and chairs. As we were driving to the rental shop, we approached the border of East Grand Rapids, an affluent community tucked alongside Grand Rapids. Quentin turned left and took a longer route, staying inside of Grand Rapids and skirting East Grand Rapids. Although the place we were heading was in Grand Rapids, the fastest route was through East Grand Rapids.

"What are you doing?" I asked. "Why didn't you go straight?"

"It's not good for me in there," he said. He was wary of driving while Black in East Grand Rapids.

"Really?" I said, slowly comprehending. "Wait a minute. Have you been pulled over in there?" I started to feel angry. This wasn't right. This was America. Any person, regardless of color, should be able to drive the most direct route through any community without consequence. I started to express my anger and Quentin just looked at me and shook his head. He smiled and I realized, although I was his Young Life supervisor, he saw more than I saw and knew more than I knew. This was more than a decade before the killings of George Floyd, Philando Castile, Breonna Taylor, and so many others would awaken our national consciousness to the dangers people of color face living their normal lives. That ride has stayed with me as an example of how markedly different my life experience as a white man is from the life experience of a person of color. For people of color, things are often not the way they should be, while white people like me move around in clueless comfort.

"White privilege" is a term that gets misunderstood. It does not mean all white people have easy lives. One of the things it means is what Quentin and I were experiencing. When we were done with the table and chairs and I was driving by myself, I would return to driving through East Grand Rapids without incident, having the privilege not to think about the color of my skin. Quentin does not have that privilege. To this day, Quentin still won't drive through East Grand Rapids, and is reminded of the color of his skin every time he goes the long way around.

$\sim$

Quentin grew up in Detroit, where he'd been a high school football star. He'd already been working with young people in and out of the church in different capacities, including coaching football, when I met him. I was impressed by his personality and call to youth ministry. I was even more impressed when I met his family. Quentin's wife, Phyllis, has a gentle, serene presence, and they had a houseful of energetic kids. Phyllis brought a daughter into the marriage, and then Quentin and Phyllis had a daughter and two sons. They were a lively bunch. One time I had an extra turkey at Thanksgiving, and we cooked it a few days after the actual holiday and invited friends over for another round of Thanksgiving dinner. The Henry family with their kids brought a wonderful energy to our home.

Quiniece was a lot like her dad. She was outgoing and animated, not afraid to be in front of an audience to speak or lead. She not only loved to have fun but could be serious as well. While her father had done better on the football field than in the classroom,

Quiniece was a good student who was not afraid of speaking up in class when she didn't understand what the teacher was saying.

"She was not like me in that regard," her father said. "I'd sit quietly and try to figure things out on my own. She was a ball of energy and always had the courage to speak up."

She loved her father's work with Young Life, often accompanying him to different events, and especially enjoyed going to camp with him. She gravitated towards those who were serving, doing menial jobs at camp, and sought to help and encourage them.

"She really did think of others first," Quentin said. "She was bright and interested in being helpful. She had a lot of me in her—maybe more than any of my other children—but she also had her mom in her. She could step away and be quiet and peaceful like her mom."

∾

Quiniece was in seventh grade when, on February 6, 2014, she complained of a stomach ache. Phyllis took her for treatment and after a round of blood tests, Phyllis was instructed to take Quiniece to the hospital, where imaging revealed she had a tumor in her stomach. Quiniece was diagnosed with Burkitt lymphoma, a fast-growing non-Hodgkin cancer. It is a treatable form of cancer, and the plan was to start chemotherapy immediately. The medical staff was optimistic Quiniece's cancer would yield to treatment. Burkitt lymphoma has a high survivability rate in young people. In typical fashion, Quiniece sought to reassure everyone things were going to be all right, telling her nurses, "It's okay, my Daddy's called Jesus about this."

As I talked to Quentin, he was reluctant to say much about what happened next, other than noting, "Quiniece had great care from dedicated nurses, but a mistake was made. Mistakes happen. My wife and I have worked very hard not to dwell on the mistake."

A *Grand Rapids Press* article on March 6, 2014, headlined "Forest Hills 13-year-old had Cancer, But Died from Accident at Hospital, Death Certificate Shows," sheds light. Quiniece Henry died on February 13, 2014, seven days after being admitted to the hospital. According to the article, "The death certificate shows she died from complications resulting from an intravascular line that caused a perforation to a chamber of her heart." The county medical examiner "noted the direct cause of death was pericardial tamponade ... the 'right atrium perforated from placement of intravascular line' and ruled the death accidental."

I reached out to Dr. Steven Orlow, a retired cardiologist who placed intravascular lines inside of patients for twenty-five years, for help understanding the medical language. He explained that Quiniece required a central venous catheter to infuse her chemo-therapy. An IV in the arm would not be adequate because the drug required dilution by large volumes of blood. That sort of volume is found in the larger veins in the vascular tree in the chest. Medical protocol calls for an X-ray after the insertion of the catheter to determine if the placement is correct. In Quiniece's case, the tip of the catheter pierced her heart. Why the catheter was not then removed is unknown. Perhaps Quiniece's X-ray wasn't conclusive, or the surgeon disagreed with the radiologist's interpretation of the X-ray.

As Dr. Orlow explained it: "The small plastic tube placed in the blood vessel in her chest to deliver chemotherapy poked a hole in the first chamber of her heart, allowing blood to leak around her heart. This blood outside her heart occupied the space normally occupied by the heart when filling with blood before each con-traction. With each beat, the heart was squeezing out to the body less and less blood until the pumping was insufficient to keep her alive." Quiniece went into cardiac arrest and the medical team was unable to resuscitate her.

"I'm not a doctor," Quentin said, "I don't understand lymphoma or the placement of catheters. I have to trust someone else. There was nothing I could do. That's paralyzing to a dad. Dads are pro-tectors, they want to love and be there and help their kids. In this situation there was nothing I could do."

~

Quiniece's funeral was an intensely sad expression of lament and grief. The funeral was held at a large nondenominational church on the same side of town as Quiniece's school. On the day of Quiniece's funeral, the sanctuary, which at that time seated over 1,400 people, was full. Quiniece's classmates attended, members of the medical staff were there, along with friends from Young Life, to rally around the Henry family. "Quiniece," her father said, "would have been happy to know the number of people her life touched."

Quiniece's body was there in an open coffin—something increasingly rare at funerals—and there was a gospel choir and multiple testimonies about her life. Quentin spoke through tears at the end of the service, citing Proverbs 3:5, "Trust in the Lord with all your heart and lean not on your own understanding," and asked those present to pray for his family because they were on a new journey. He said that they had lost a jewel and that the life of their family would be forever changed.

I remember being emotionally spent. I had wept continuously for over two hours. I wasn't alone. A lot of Kleenex was used in the sanctuary that day. It was just so sad. I no longer worked for Young Life in 2014, and didn't see the Henrys as much, but I remembered Quiniece as a young woman with so much vitality. The tragic nature of her death seemed unfathomable.

I also remember hugging Quentin after the service. I was undone, a total wreck, and he kept telling me it was going to be okay.

Why was he comforting me?

Like Roger Nelson, Quentin Henry demonstrates extraordinary resilience.

~

As we talked about what people said to him in the days immediately following Quiniece's death, Quentin mentioned many positive expressions of empathy. He also recalled some that were not helpful. People occasionally blundered—most notably he remembered someone trying to comfort him by pointing out that he had other children who were still alive.

"The Lord helped me be gracious," Quentin said, "and not dwell on those kinds of crazy comments. You just have to stand there and take it—just have to let people say what they're going to say. I know they're trying, and their hearts are good, but sometimes people's hearts and words don't line up. Being mature means seeing people's hearts and allowing them to say whatever it is they're going to say. What mattered most, though, was not people's words, but the fact that they showed up and put their love and care into action."

Then he thought for a moment, laughed, and said, "I don't think we made a meal for a year because of all the food friends provided. It got to be so much that I had to ask my partner, Fred, and his wife to help coordinate everything."

The Young Life Committee, a group typically made up of parents and Young Life alumni who provide support in several ways for the ministry, arranged for the Henry family to go to Alongside Ministries, a retreat center near Kalamazoo, Michigan, that helps people in ministry facing crises. The school system allowed

Quiniece's younger brothers to attend school virtually, and the family stayed at the Alongside Ministries retreat center for about three months. Sessions with individual counselors and family therapists helped the healing process. It was important, Quentin said, for people to say to him that they understood his situation and that they wanted him to be with his family.

"I had been focused so much on making sure my wife and kids were all right," Quentin said, "that I really hadn't digested it for myself. I had to look at it and face the reality that I had lost not only a daughter, but a confidante and a friend. Quiniece would always ask me how my day was and showed real curiosity and interest in my ministry. Now she was gone. The journey made me ask what I really believed. I wondered how to navigate this. People would say, 'Do you still go to church? You lost a loved one. Why do you still have a smile on your face? How come you're still praying and helping people?'"

Why did he remain active in the church? "I just looked around and saw people were still in need. My daughter had been in need. We were in need. The only one I can run to is not myself but Christ. When I don't have any place to go, I go to him. He is my rock. My caregiver. Without Christ, I would have lost my mind. That's not an exaggeration. I wouldn't be able to function. Or be around young people. Every single time I see a young woman around Quiniece's age, I think of her. It makes me sad. But I also have joy—a lot of joy, in telling people not to take your kids for granted. They're precious. Life is precious. The pandemic has reinforced that life is fleeting—you can be here today and gone tomorrow. Don't take life and those you love for granted. Life sure isn't about working endless hours so you can accumulate stuff. It's not about having a title or a lot of money. It's about loving those around you, about how much love you have around you."

The loss was nearly overwhelming. "There's so much about Quiniece's life I was looking forward to. She wanted to go to college, and own her own business, have her own shop and make jewelry. I wondered who she would marry. Her death leaves a hole, a hole in my life, a hole in my heart. I know I need to stay the course, but I feel that hole. I think about her every day."

Quiniece's story is complicated by race. There is no question that people of color have disproportionate negative outcomes in the American health care system. The U.S. Centers for Disease Control and Prevention explains:

> Racism—both interpersonal and structural—negatively affects the mental and physical health of millions of people, preventing them from attaining their highest level of health, and consequently, affecting the health of our nation. A growing body of research shows that centuries of racism in this country has had a profound and negative impact on communities of color. The impact is pervasive and deeply embedded in our society—affecting where one lives, learns, works, worships, and plays and creating inequities in access to a range of social and economic benefits—such as housing, education, wealth, and employment. These conditions—often referred to as social determinants of health—are key drivers of health inequities within communities of color, placing those within these populations at greater risk for poor health outcomes.

I asked Quentin what role race might have played in Quiniece's death.

"Death does not care what color you are," he said. "Death is equal opportunity; death comes for us all. It's true that stuff like this happens all the time to people of color. I don't know why injustice is out of hand. But I'm not going to focus on that. My focus is on God, and I have asked God: What do I need to learn as a man, as a father, as a husband, as a believer? I have concluded God wants me to trust him and not make excuses. I'm not going to give the power that belongs to God to people. What matters for me is how I respond, what matters are the choices I make. It would be very possible for me and my family to get stuck on and in Quiniece's death. We could easily become angry, resentful, bitter people, paralyzed because something horrible happened to a member of our family. But we choose not to be that way. We have put our trust in God, even when outcomes aren't the ones we would want.

"That's not to diminish the injustice in our racially imbalanced healthcare system. Black families have suffered. My family has suffered. And there is a lot of injustice we should be angry about—things like generational poverty and hunger. I saw someone on TV the other day who owned three hundred cars. We should be sad and upset about that, not celebrating it. But I am not angry about what happened to Quiniece. What good would that do? It wouldn't change anything. It would only hurt and diminish me. I try to be level-headed. Life is reciprocal. If we give anger, we get anger back. If we give love, we get love back. If we are fair, we get fair treatment back. I'm not angry, but I am disappointed when I am not treated reciprocally."

Quentin and Phyllis eventually reached a settlement with the hospital, the details of which have not been publicly released. Mainly, Quentin and Phyllis simply wanted to move on. Quentin said, "It's a great hospital that helps a lot of people and people should not be afraid to bring their kids there. I'm at peace with what happened. It was a mistake, plain and simple, that no one wanted."

Because he is a person of faith, people do occasionally ask Quentin why he thinks this happened to his daughter.

Quentin says he refuses to dwell on that question. "Look at me—I am a Black man trying to live an upright life, doing the Lord's work, working with kids, working in the church. So, why should this happen to my family? It's okay to question God, but

I'm not going to lose my faith because tragedy comes. Tragedy hits everyone, no matter what. Why should my position or faith make me immune? I trust that God has things under control. I don't have a crystal ball. I can't see everything God can see. I cannot tell you why this happened, but I can tell you that it has grounded me. I would never choose this, never in a million years. I know some people experience loss and spiral into depression and anger and never recover. Instead, they share their pain with everyone. I want to still love people. I want to share my experience and help people see the importance of their loved ones and the importance of cherishing the time we have with them. We have to know how to love and forgive each other, how to be honest and transparent with each other. We need to be humble. We need to be able to say, 'I'm sorry, I'm still learning, I'm still growing.' The number one thing I have learned from this is to take time to slow down and love those in my circle. That's Quiniece's legacy."

I processed Quentin and Quiniece's story with Marilyn McEntyre, who taught medical humanities in the joint medical schools of the University of California Berkeley and the University of California San Francisco for several years. She is a prolific writer, and her book *Dear Doctor*, published in 2021, is written in the form of a letter from a patient to a doctor, exploring the needs and fears we bring into the offices of medical professionals. She has also served as a hospice volunteer and used those experiences when writing her books, *A Faithful Farewell*, about dying well, and *A Long Letting Go*, for families in the process of losing a loved one. As a writer and professor of literature, she cares deeply about words, and we started with the meaning of words before going specifically into the Henry family's story.

"Sorrow is a large word," Marilyn said, "larger than sadness. Sadness is an emotion, but sometimes it's helpful to think of sorrow as a place you go. It's similar to what Flannery O'Connor said about sickness—that sickness is a place you go and nobody can follow you. Sorrow is also place you go on your own journey, but others are there. It's a pool you step into that other people are in. Sorrow is a shared space that becomes more familiar as you get older, because if you live long enough you inevitably have losses. Increasingly, I feel as though sorrow is a part of our contract with God: We come here on this assignment, this journey, and part of the territory we've agreed to walk through is the vale of tears, the valley of the shadow of death. God will be with us, but we won't be spared sorrow. I have appreciated the opportunity through hospice to be reflective about what it means to walk alongside others in sorrow, and to learn what it means to bear witness or to be willing to witness someone's sorrow. As you do that, the question that naturally arises is, 'How do you process your own sorrow?'

"Here are a few things I've learned processing loss: First, grief takes you by surprise. As much as I appreciate the efforts people have made to name and identify stages of grief, I don't trust 'staging.' Things happen the way they happen. An analogy has been made to the stages of labor, but after giving birth to three children I'd say the idea that there are stages of labor is laughable. Obstetrics is full of surprises. So also with grief. Grief doesn't take a foreordained course. It's going to be a thread in your life story, not an event. I still miss my mother, even though it's been years since she died. It's not as though I can say, 'That happened, I had a mother, she lived a good long life, she died, now I'm over the loss of her.' Grief doesn't go away; sorrow is one measure of the value of what has departed from our lives. I talk with people whose loved one, like my mother, lived a good long life and they wonder if they have a right to grieve because 'it was time' for their loved one to die. But we all have a right to grief."

As Marilyn spoke of grief taking us by surprise, I thought of the first line of C.S. Lewis' book *A Grief Observed*: "No one ever told me grief felt so like fear." There's irony in that the person who wrote *Surprised by Joy* was also surprised by grief. In Lewis' case, I don't think grief felt *like* fear, I think it *was* fear. The loss of his wife completely unsettled him and thrust him into an unknown future. Fear is a normal response to the unknown.

"Another way grief may take you by surprise," Marilyn said, "is by bringing shame with it. When my mother died, all I could think of was the times I didn't go see her. Or maybe a husband feels as though he's supposed to be a protector and can't save his wife from the disease that takes her life. He sees the loss, perhaps irrationally, as his failure. Grief can be hard for men in a particular way because we live with old cultural assumptions that grief is women's work.

"Another thing about grief, as my husband has pointed out, is that every new sorrow triggers memories of previous losses. Sorrow is kind of a palimpsest or fugue. One sorrow reawakens another. Thinking about the death of Quiniece Henry brings up not only all the deaths in the Henry family, but the medical carelessness around African American people—even if the cause of Quiniece's death was an honest medical mistake. The history of medical care of Black people in this country is horrific. They've been experimented upon, they've been neglected, they've been lied to. What has happened under the banner of medicine has to give the Black community pause. There are large cultural dimensions to this story, and, as this story illustrates, sorrow and loss are never singular. That's why I like the image of stepping into a pool or stepping into a river of sorrow on whose shores we all live. We step in at a particular place because our losses are very particular. But our specific loss is part of something larger—we discover others are there. Healing comes as we widen the lens and take in the reality that loss is something many others have experienced. My pain is my pain, but it is also something that links me to others in a deep and irreducible way."

Marilyn mentioned healing, and I wondered since there are so many aspects to sorrow and grief, what it means to heal from grief. What does healing look like? Marilyn spoke of growing around the loss: Just as a tree grows around a wound and the rings assume a new shape, so also our lives are shaped by our losses.

"Grief does not go away," she said, "but we can heal from the immediacy of rending grief. We will go on and function and it can become part of a story that has a lot of grace and goodness and even laughter in it. Still, it's important to recognize that it's never going to go away. We never forget."

She spoke also of the etymology of the word grief, which comes from an old French word for burden. It is linguistically related to the Latin word *gravis*, meaning weighty, the root of "gravity" and "gravitas" and "grave." Thinking of grief as a burden indicates it is something we carry.

"We learn to shoulder heavier burdens as we move into maturity," Marilyn said. "There's a certain way we grow into grief and become able to carry it. All of the words we use—sorrow, loss, weight, burden, depression, sadness, darkness—have histories that invite us into reflection. We tend to use them interchangeably, but they have nuances that aren't interchangeable. Sorrow, for example, is dignified. As I said, sorrow is not the same as sadness. It is also not the same as depression. Sorrow has a spiritual dimension to it that depression does not necessarily have. People say, 'I'm so depressed,' when often what they mean is 'I am sad,' or 'I am both sad and angry.' The word 'depression' is part of the language of psychology. Psychological words are helpful for naming things, but sometimes they may divert us from both the spiritual and historical dimensions of what we're experiencing. Psychology has given us helpful terms for naming particular pathologies, but I am troubled when those words displace language that leads us into the deeper waters of spirituality."

~

When I asked what stood out specifically in the story of Quentin and Quiniece, Marilyn spoke first of the danger of compartmentalizing stories.

"The temptation," she said, "is to classify a story, to say, 'this story is about a medical mistake' or 'this story is about spirituality,' or 'this story is about racial injustice.' We compartmentalize stories, and in doing so we tidy them up, separating the conditions of someone's life from the particular events. That's too sanitizing. The Henry family's story opens into questions about so many things: about what faith looks like, about being Black in America, about medical error, about the legal system, but also about the conditions in which people are damaged and get help. In the same way that every grief brings up other griefs, every injury to a Black person triggers awareness of all the injuries that have been inflicted on and occurred at the expense of African Americans. The fact that the Henrys are an African American family is inseparable from the way the story unfolds. We assume it turns on an honest medical mistake, but as with every other institution in America, the people of conscience in American medicine, practicing physicians and medical historians, are increasingly publicly coming to terms with inequities in medicine and what has disproportionately happened to Black bodies.

"When I was teaching premed students in a class on writing and medical life, I put a sentence on the board that said, 'Every health issue is a public health issue.' They had to write about that. Here's an example: Let's say someone comes in with a broken bone. In what circumstances did this person break the bone? Let's say it happened riding a bike. How much protection did they have? How old was the bike? Where was the pothole? All of that is part of what happened. I wanted them to see the person with a broken bone as part of larger intersecting systems. One of the first things to say about the Henrys' story is it is part of larger systems in which outcomes are still significantly variable.

"When I think of what stands out in their story, I want to mention the funeral, and the intense emotionality of it. The community surrounding the Henrys is an important part of the story. The Black Church has historically been the 'beloved community' of which Martin Luther King spoke. There is a skill involved in being a community that can hold people in their sorrows. There's a skill involved in being those women who bring spices to the tomb or the ladies who bring casseroles to the funeral or the hospice people who sit at the bedside or stand at the side of the room while the family gathers and doesn't know what to do. There are people who know how to stand with others in their grief. I am reminded of something Tom Gillespie said when he was president of Princeton Theological Seminary: 'Thank God for the Black Church in America. They know things white churches need to learn.' Every time I visit an African American church I am humbled by the hospitality and open-heartedness and capacity to embrace other people's life conditions. White people talk about being inclusive—maybe we should talk more about being included. For white people inclusiveness often means, 'You get to come into our circle.' Instead, sometimes it should be, 'Can we apply to come into your circle? Can we knock on your door and learn from you?' How you confront and walk through and share your own loss, rending pain and grief, is a witness. It's something the Black Church does well."

Marilyn spoke of the character Dilsey in William Faulkner's *The Sound and the Fury*. Dilsey is the Black cook and loyal servant of a highly dysfunctional white family. In the final section of the book, Dilsey goes to church and weeps. "Over the years, I've thought a lot about Dilsey's tears," Marilyn said. "The Black Church provides a safe space where Dilsey can sit down and cry. The Black Church is a place where she can be uplifted in song and held in her sorrows. A place where everyone knows and understands. This is a place where someone can just sit down and weep."

Marilyn also was struck by Quentin's statement: "I am not a doctor." She said, "I find that very poignant. How many things are silenced behind that statement? People disempower themselves when they walk into a physician's office. Those white coats are a barrier, often a protective barrier. We violate all sorts of social protocols in a doctor's office; we disrobe, making us very vulnerable, and talk to someone we typically don't know well about the most intimate things. All the while we're in an environment of institutional sterility that makes it less of a human encounter. Yet we are asked to trust."

There is poignancy in the parallel lines of trust in this story. Quentin had to trust the doctors to take care of his daughter. At the same time, he trusted God with his daughter. Quentin's understanding and experience with trust runs not just through this story but through the rest of his life as well.

~

I was eager to get Marilyn's insights into the medical community's role in Quiniece's case. What does a tragedy like this feel like from that point of view? How do doctors deal with making mistakes?

"Some hospitals," Marilyn said, "are starting to use a systems approach to medical error instead of simply identifying who put the needle in the arm or administered the wrong pill. They are stepping back and asking, 'What is it about the way things happen in this hospital that allowed this to happen? What are the checkpoints?' The systems approach doesn't go to personal blame immediately. They're focused on figuring out the structural flaws that, for instance, make it possible for someone to be so tired when they are on duty that they miss things, or identify why the person who handed the surgeon the incorrect line was distracted. Exploring medical history also helps look at medical error in a larger context, not searching for excuses, but to say it is never sufficient to pin the error on someone's inexperience or inattention or carelessness.

"Every doctor I know really cares about doing the job right. I once attended a conference on medical error and one of the things that arose was how much guilt doctors carry when there has been an error. There's little they can do with their guilt because historically hospitals have prohibited doctors from asking for forgiveness. Many still do. Asking for forgiveness is prohibited because it constitutes an admission of guilt that opens the hospital to litigation. Our litigious environment means everybody ends up damaged.

"I have a friend whose husband died due to medical error. She went with good will to the hospital in the middle of her grief because she wanted the story. She asked, 'Can I just get the story, so I know what happened to him that day? What happened in the recovery room—because that was where he died.' They wouldn't give her the information. She finally sued. She didn't want a lawsuit, she said, but that was the only way to get the story.

"The guilt doctors carry, their own sorrow, drives many of them into depression and to suicide. The suicide rate among doctors is astonishingly high. There's a lot of pressure on them and a lot of perfectionism in that profession. They are doing high-risk things, and if a doctor does the wrong thing to the wrong person at the wrong time, that doctor is going to take a big hit and maybe even lose their career. I sometimes wonder why people go into high-risk medical specialties like surgery. Someone at the conference said, 'We just pray that when we make an error it will be small and correctible, because we all make errors.' The margin for error allowed to doctors is very narrow. That gives me a lot of sympathy for the predicament that doctors, as well as patients, are in with a system that doesn't provide space for processing grief on either side.

"Some hospitals are experimenting with mediation. In some ways, it's similar to the Truth and Reconciliation Commission that was convened to address the wounds of apartheid in South Africa. Families like the Henrys, who have been damaged by a medical error, can agree to meet with the medical professionals involved and with a mediator, to talk with each other, express the depth of their loss, maybe their anger, but also, as with my friend who just wanted to know the story, find out what actually happened and receive an authentic apology. To hear someone say, 'I would give anything if I could take this back,' goes further than people might think. To the degree that our healthcare institutions start experimenting with how forgiveness happens, they can recover some health in a very broken system."

There is no question a process like that would be beneficial to the Henrys. Although Quentin is reluctant to speak of his dealings with the hospital, my sense is that meeting the physician whose mistake ended Quiniece's life and hearing an apology would bring great healing. Instead, the Henry family's only avenue of recourse was the legal system, which, as in the case of Roger Nelson, can be retraumatizing. Wounds that are in the process of being healed are reopened. Roger's case was in the criminal justice system; the Henry's case would be in the civil justice system.

One example of how the civil justice system can retraumatize is found in the Doctrine of Comparative Responsibility. This is a feature in civil law which assesses the responsibility of each party in a lawsuit. Plaintiffs receive only the percentage of an award they are not responsible for. In other words, if attorneys can establish that the plaintiffs hold 25% of the responsibility, the hospital only pays 75% of the ordered award. That becomes significant when there are millions of dollars at stake. This means there are huge financial incentives for hospital attorneys to aggressively go after people who have suffered egregiously, asserting the negligence of those seeking justice and healing.

"We have a son who was a public defender and has shared about the underside of the justice system," Marilyn said. "I can say that the justice system frequently doesn't offer justice. On top of that, a more complex goal like healing is simply beyond its reach. The systemic issues in both medicine and law can be looked at analogously. The law is supposed to provide safety and a measure of protection—but often it doesn't. Getting a big settlement—which in my opinion the Henrys are entitled to—shouldn't be a pyrrhic victory. This story is one of many that should be told as part of a larger public story so we can imagine ourselves into more healing and healthier medical and justice systems."

Marilyn's comments raise questions about restorative justice and forgiveness. After a career spent working in nonprofits, I know firsthand that institutional administrators feel more pressure to protect and preserve their institutions than to ask profound questions about the nature of justice and what institutional forgiveness might look like. In my career, when difficult situations arose, our first call was not to a philosopher or ethicist or theologian who could help us think deeply about justice (and, when I worked at a seminary, those people were in the building). We called our attorney, who worked to protect the institution.

More than half of the hospitals in the U.S. are nonprofits, and hospital administrators are accountable to boards of trustees, made up of wealthy people who have a fiduciary responsibility as trustees. Like many mature nonprofits, hospitals have large endowments, sometimes not just in millions, but billions of dollars. Those assets are inviting targets for the unscrupulous and I have sympathy for the pressures faced by institutions. Ultimately, though, institutions are made up of people. Imagine the emotional and spiritual consequences for the doctor whose error killed Quiniece Henry. I wonder if there could have been a route that offered forgiveness and healing, not just for the Henrys, but for the doctor also. What would it take for institutions to see that the sort of mediation Marilyn mentioned is not only in the interest of the aggrieved family, but in the interest of the institution as well?

~

As I reflected on the way Quentin told his story, I was struck by how often he would say something like, "I won't get stuck there." Many elements in the story present challenges that he perceived as holes he could fall into and become trapped in bitterness and anger. He could be trapped in the medical error, trapped in how race complicates everything, even trapped in the horrifically insensitive comment that he should cheer up because he had other children at home. He refuses to do that. I asked Marilyn what she made of this.

"I understand why that is important to Quentin personally," she said. "His desire not to get trapped in bitterness or anger or resentment is admirable. It's very difficult to find the line between being generous, welcoming, accepting, and forgiving on the one hand, and acknowledging profound injustice on the other. There's a place for outrage. Injustice needs to be named, though perhaps not always by the most injured party. Part of holding grief in community is that others might pick up that piece of the burden and speak out on behalf of the family. Quiniece's story brings up so many factors around it: litigiousness, greed, the unforgiving nature of institutions—all those aspects need to be named. Her story shouldn't just go underground."

Finally, there's that frequently mentioned element of trust. In a later chapter, there's the story of another parent who has lost a child and says, "I still trust God, but I don't trust God to keep my children safe."

I asked Marilyn what it means to trust God after the horrific happens: "A friend said something about trust that has stayed with me. She said when you trust someone you don't trust 'that,' you trust 'them.' You don't trust *that* they won't do something that hurts you. You trust *them*—even when those things happen, who they are is still something you can invest your trust in. Who rather than what is what matters. Having said that, I believe trusting God has much to do with my conviction that life is a journey, or, as I sometimes say, that we are on assignment here. What we see is not the whole story. We go through things here, and then we get to go home."

Her words echo Paul's famous words in I Corinthians 13: Now we see in a mirror dimly; then we will see face to face.

"It's helpful to step back," Marilyn said, "and widen the frame and say, 'There is a much bigger story that I am a part of. God has offered me this time on earth, and I will more fully understand what it's about when it's over.' In the middle of it, we know bad things are going to happen. That's part of the deal. If our trust in God is based on bad things not happening, our trust is pretty fragile. It's hard to move from trusting in the sense of feeling protected to trusting in the way that says finally, 'I know in whom I have believed.' Anyone you love will disappoint you at certain times. But love is resilient. That's not in I Corinthians 13, but it should be: Love is patient, love is kind, love is resilient ... Love says, 'I trust you, we'll move through this, and we'll move beyond it.' A lot of Christian theology overemphasizes God's imminence and forgets God's transcendence and sovereignty."

God's imminence means that God is not only real, but perceivable and knowable. Leaning too far in that direction leads to thinking and speaking of God in personal and private terms. The wholly other God, creator of the universe, gets reduced to a good luck charm that can be carried in one's pocket. By emphasizing God's transcendence and sovereignty, we are affirming the universe is much bigger than simply "Me and Jesus."

"The sense of how big the universe is that astronomy provides is helpful," Marilyn said. "I love that T-shirt that has a picture of the Milky Way on it with a little arrow that says, 'You are here.' We are part of something so much bigger than the immediacies of our lives. All the pain and all the suffering is part of something that we don't have the perspective to see. Reframing our stories—even a story as sad and tragic as Quiniece's—to see a bigger picture is helpful. Quentin understands this."

Finally, I asked about the idea of the stewardship of pain. Marilyn spoke again of the importance of telling Quiniece's story, how telling the story is being a steward of it. "If my husband dies first," she said, "or one of the children, I think all I'm going to want to do is burrow. I am sure some part of the Henrys just wants to do that, to be unseen and get on with their lives. Yet we encourage each other when we tell our stories. A story like Quiniece's deserves to have a spotlight shone on it. The fact that Quentin has been through this becomes one of the things he—along with his wife and other children—bears into the world.

"A few years ago I was co-leading a prayer retreat and we asked the participants 'What are the gifts you bring to the community?' We were asking not just about their talents, but how the community would be enriched because they were present. I remember one older woman simply said, 'I've been through things.' I loved that response. We need people among us who have been through things and are willing to show up. The Henrys have been through this, and they're showing up."

One way the Henrys are faithful with Quiniece's story is simply by sharing it. The hospital has every reason not to want it told. But it is a story much larger than the medical error. It is a story of faith, love, anguish, error, the quest for healing and forgiveness, race, grief, community, sorrow, hope, and resilience.

Quentin Henry has worked in youth ministry in West Michigan for over twenty-five years. Currently, he serves as a specialist in a residential care facility with adolescents who have gone through significant trauma.

Marilyn McEntyre is a teacher and writer who has taught medical humanities and written more than twenty books. www.MarilynMcEntyre.com

5

A Mysterious Grace Shines Through

"People would say, 'Why don't you do this?' or 'Come be with these people so you won't be lonely.' I wanted to be lonely. I wanted to step into the loss, see what it was like, and see what God would do."
Cancer caregiver Mary Anderson

"God never promises to take away suffering. It's our witness and presence in the midst of suffering that shows our character."
Cancer survivor Mitch Kinsinger

Mitch and Sandie Kinsinger's story is a cancer story, and it is like so many other cancer stories—a story of life and death and suffering. But there are ways Mitch and Sandie's story is unique. Their story raises questions about the amount of suffering humans can tolerate.

I remember exactly when I first met Mitch—and also clearly remember I wasn't inclined to like him very much. It was at a Young Life leadership camp in 1983. Mitch was a Wheaton College student, good looking, tall, and full of charisma. He played basketball and football at Wheaton.

Why didn't I like him? Envy. He was everything I dreamt of being but wasn't. But then one night we had a talent show and Mitch walked onto the stage with his guitar and sang a soulful rendition of Simon and Garfunkel's "Homeward Bound," and I found my eyes filling with tears and my heart melting. I had no way of knowing then how our paths would continuously cross over the coming decades. We became friends, and remain friends, almost forty years later.

Mitch was a farm boy, raised Mennonite in a rural community in southeastern Iowa. He grew up embracing the Mennonite traditions of nonviolence, simplicity, peace, and justice. He went to a Mennonite high school and graduated with a sense that the purpose of his life should be to help others in the name of Jesus.

Wheaton was an adjustment—not just away from his Mennonite background into the heart of American Evangelicalism, but also away from his rural roots into a campus filled with kids from upper-middle-class white suburbia. Mitch adjusted, although what had been common-sense wisdom in the Mennonite world became rules at Wheaton—and woe to those who broke the rules!

One day during his senior year, Mitch was in a friend's apartment playing the guitar when someone heard him and asked him to play for a local Young Life club. Mitch was interested in youth ministry and so he agreed, and before long discovered a specific vocational direction. He joined the staff of Young Life after he graduated from Wheaton.

He also met Sandie Hoover at Wheaton. Mitch became aware of Sandie because one of Mitch's best friends was also named Hoover, and after that friend saw Sandie's picture in the student directory, he jokingly said to Mitch, "Leave my sister alone." Mitch and Sandie were in a psychology class together and would see each other on campus but hadn't met. That changed one weekend when the school tradition was that girls would ask guys out on dates. One of Sandie's friends asked Mitch out on her behalf, and Mitch and

Sandie began dating. They had different experiences at Wheaton, "I went to Wheaton and it was a move to a more conservative ethos than I was used to," Mitch said. "Sandie went to Wheaton and it was a move to a more liberal ethos than she was used to."

They were married in May 1985. Young Life used to hold summer training seminars for its staff in my hometown of Holland, Michigan, in the mid-1980s. The classes were held at Western Theological Seminary and families were housed at Hope College. After their honeymoon, Mitch and Sandie came to Holland to attend Young Life classes. Mitch was in town when my fiancée, Gretchen, had her stroke in July of 1985, and is one of the people who reached out to me during that difficult time.

In 1989, after five years with Young Life in the Chicago suburbs, Mitch and Sandie came back to Holland. Mitch enrolled as a student at Western seminary, which meant we would see each other regularly. During the years Mitch had worked for Young Life, Sandie had gotten a master's degree in art therapy at the University of Illinois Chicago and got a job doing art therapy at Pine Rest Christian Mental Health Services in Grand Rapids. They became head residents in a Hope College residence hall, and Mitch worked odd jobs like delivering packages for UPS while finishing his degree at Western. The plan all along was for Mitch to eventually go to graduate school, and after graduating from Western he was accepted into a Ph.D. program at the University of Iowa. Their family, bolstered by the birth of two sons in Holland, moved to a farmhouse not far from where Mitch had grown up. He studied American religious history at Iowa.

Sometime during those years our family stopped for a night in that farmhouse on our way to Colorado for Christmas. This was pre-GPS and the streets didn't have street signs. The directions, which included turning right at a manure spreader, live on in our family lore. It was a typical December Iowa night of clear skies and bone-rattling cold. The top floor of the house didn't have heat—only holes cut in the floor to let the first floor's heat rise. It didn't seem to me that much hot air bothered to make its way upstairs—it took incredible amounts of resolve to get out of our warm bed covers in the morning.

The Kinsingers spent eight years in Iowa. Another son was born and Mitch plugged away at his degree. Sandie worked in a number of different social service agencies, primarily focusing on at-risk kids. At times Sandie was supporting Mitch's academic career, at other times Mitch put school on hold and took care of the kids while Sandie worked. In 2000, Mitch accepted a faculty position at Northwestern College in Orange City, Iowa, the same small Reformed Church in America school at which Ron Nelson, whose story was told earlier in this book, had taught. Over the years at Northwestern, Mitch finished his Ph.D. and moved up the academic ladder from being an assistant professor to eventually holding an endowed chair in the religion department. Sandie was also hired by Northwestern, first as an adjunct teaching art therapy and developmental psychology, and then to a full-time faculty position. She also earned a Ph.D. in educational psychology at the University of South Dakota. Her dissertation topic was the psychology of hope.

∼

I hadn't seen Mitch and Sandie in years when I was invited to speak in chapel at Northwestern in 2010. Although Mitch and I had spoken from time to time, I had it in my head that Mitch was a professor and Sandie a therapist. It hadn't fully registered with me until I saw them that there were two Dr. Kinsingers in the family. I heard from the college's chaplain, who had invited me there, that Sandie was a much-esteemed professor. As Mitch put it, "Sandie juggled so many commitments and responsibilities in her professional and personal career. She was a mentor for high school and college students, adjusted to a variety of jobs, became a phenomenal teacher, and was a great mom who was always there for our boys."

Part of what made her a phenomenal teacher were all the different jobs Sandie had held in various agencies and psychiatric hospitals in Chicago, Grand Rapids, and Iowa. She had an endless supply of stories because she'd seen most everything in the world of social services. All those different positions, which had seemed like a drag as Mitch and Sandie were just trying to make ends meet, served her well. She thrived as a professor at Northwestern.

Mitch, however, eventually grew restless. As his academic career developed, he did more administrative work and found it rewarding to think about the big picture of the work of the college. After fifteen years at Northwestern, he accepted a position as associate vice president for academic affairs at Augustana University in Sioux Falls, South Dakota. After commuting for a year, the Kinsingers moved to Sioux Falls in 2016, and Sandie joined the faculty at Augustana, teaching developmental and educational psychology. Mitch was happy working on curriculum, faculty development, assessment, and accreditation. He enjoyed focusing on keeping the wheels of academia moving and freeing Augustana's faculty members from bureaucracy so they could focus on teaching.

But Mitch didn't feel great physically. He felt like something was off, even though the former Wheaton College athlete was still in good shape. Early in 2018, an ultrasound revealed Mitch's abdomen was full of enlarged cancerous lymph nodes. He was diagnosed with follicular lymphoma.

In the cancer lottery, follicular lymphoma tends to be a winning ticket. It is an indolent form of cancer, meaning it grows very slowly, and people can live with it undetected for years. It kills some people, yet others with follicular lymphoma never require treatment and eventually die from some other cause. There are spectrums of intensity within different cancer diagnoses, and although Mitch's cancer had developed and required treatment, his doctor said there was no reason to believe they would have started treatment if the cancer had been discovered earlier. Mitch had a regimen of chemotherapy—one treatment a month—for six months. The chemo was targeted specifically at the lymph nodes and Mitch tolerated the chemo well. He didn't lose his hair, never was a hospital in-patient, and only felt fatigued for a couple of days after each treatment. Six months later, in August of 2018, he felt better than he had in years. His scans were clear and the doctor said although follicular lymphoma is not curable and would most likely return, it would lie indolent again for years, maybe even for a decade, and then, when it did return, would likely yield again to treatment. The doctor was upbeat and said this is something Mitch would live with and not die from. Mitch likened it to having diabetes, which must be taken seriously, but can be managed with the proper treatment and care.

But by January, 2019, Mitch didn't feel well again. His doctor was skeptical the follicular lymphoma could have returned so soon. Tests were run and unfortunately the doctor was correct—the follicular lymphoma had not returned. Instead, Mitch had diffuse large B-cell lymphoma, a much more aggressive form of lymphoma. No one could say if the follicular lymphoma had morphed into this or if he'd simply had both cancers at the same time and the first treatment had kept the more serious cancer at bay for a while. Perhaps the chemo from the first treatment had somehow spurred the more aggressive cancer. Aggressive cancer requires aggressive treatment, and after getting a second opinion at the Mayo Clinic, Mitch started a ninety-day regimen of very intense chemotherapy in March 2019. He was hospitalized for each round of treatment for a week or two and suffered the usual ravages of chemo. His hair fell out and he felt overwhelming fatigue. Chemo wreaks havoc in many parts of the body, including all parts of the gastrointestinal tract. Mitch's mouth became extremely sensitive. He remembers eating a banana during this time and feeling like it was covered in hot sauce. He lived on cottage cheese and applesauce and was hospitalized for fifty days of the ninety-day treatment period. Complications arose: Mitch contracted neutropenic fever, which comes from a compromised immune system, and his temperature spiked to 105 degrees. The hospital room thermostat was turned to 60 and Mitch was packed in ice to reduce the fever. He could have lost his life then but pulled through. Still, the most dramatic phase of his treatment was ahead of him.

In July 2019, Mitch went to the Holden Comprehensive Cancer Center at the University of Iowa for a stem cell transplant. He had an autologous stem cell transplant, meaning his own stem cells were harvested and used in the treatment. He was told the treatment was all or nothing—either it would kill Mitch or kill the cancer. He was hospitalized for three agonizing weeks, and then released for what would be several months of recovery. "I was masked and practicing social distancing before it was cool," Mitch said. "I just wanted to lie low and avoid infections and recover. Unfortunately, things didn't work out that way."

Sandie was flourishing professionally. As part of her work at Augustana, she was leading a research program working with pregnant women at the Cheyenne River Sioux Reservation. The subject of the study was inherited trauma, researching how decades of oppression adversely affected both women during pregnancy and the prenatal health of their babies. Yet as she was doing this, she also was not feeling well. At the same time that Mitch's second cancer appeared, she went to the doctor. Her gall bladder was removed in January 2019, but following the surgery she did not show the improvement that her physician expected. She clearly was not well, and one night in the winter of 2019, Mitch took her into the emergency room. Blood tests revealed something was wrong and she was admitted into the hospital. After a week's stay, she was diagnosed with myelodysplastic syndrome (MDS), also called pre-leukemia. MDS is a rare and serious form of cancer. Like Mitch, Sandie would require a stem cell transplant, but unlike Mitch, hers would require stem cells from a donor, since the cancer was in her blood.

Fifty percent of those who have Sandie's treatment survive for five years. Both Mitch and Sandie were staring their mortality head-on, and they accepted that the window of their time together had grown much narrower. They talked about what life would be like if one of them died. Their sense was if either of them was going to die soon, it would be Mitch. His treatment was all or nothing. On the other hand, they believed that Sandie's diagnosis meant her lifespan would be shortened, but, if Mitch survived, they would still have another five or ten years together.

Sandie's stem cell transplant was also done at the University of Iowa, on August 8, 2019, one month after Mitch's, in the same hospital wing with the same team of nurses. Mitch was recovering at his cousin's home in Iowa City. The Kinsinger's youngest son, Stefan, was the donor for Sandie's stem cell transplant. The family talked about what a great story this was going to be: Sandie had given Stefan life, and now Stefan was giving Sandie life. Reality, though, has a way of ruining great stories.

Twelve days after her stem cell transplant, Sandie developed a Clostridium difficile infection, known as C. diff. It can be devastating for patients to develop hospital-acquired infections like C. diff—the very place that is supposed to be making you well can make you sick. C. diff is highly communicable. On August 21, Mitch was called and told Sandie was being transferred into intensive care. Mitch was very ill himself but went to see Sandie. Like everyone entering Sandie's room, Mitch had to suit up in a mask and gown—C. diff could kill him.

Sandie recognized Mitch and was alert enough to comment on a new hat he was wearing. The physicians were calm and said that, although Sandie's condition was serious, they could treat it. She was injected with antibiotics yet continued to decline through the night. She was put on a ventilator, yet no matter what treatment was tried, Sandie did not respond. During the night, Mitch was asked if Sandie would want to be kept alive in a vegetative state, which Mitch knew she did not want. At 4 a.m., the medical team decided to stop treatment. Mitch was in the room when Sandie died at 6:20 a.m. on August 22, 2019. She was 57 years old.

"I trust somehow through the Spirit Sandie knew she wasn't alone when she died," Mitch said. "The day was dawning when Sandie passed, and there was a gorgeous sunrise out the window as she breathed her last. It felt cruelly ironic."

Mitch telephoned members of their family. Then he went back to his cousin's house. Suddenly, he found himself a widower, physically wasted and emotionally wrung out, faced with somehow recovering from his own stem cell transplant as he mourned his wife's death.

~

Because he was immunocompromised, Mitch spent the next few months alone. The symptoms of recovering from a stem cell transplant and grieving are the same. He was fatigued and lacked energy, was forgetful, and overwhelmingly sad.

"Yet even though I couldn't be out and about," Mitch said, "I had my phone and I had email and texts. I sat alone in my chair but was in contact with many family and friends—a great cloud of witnesses—who supported me. I just tried to survive, to put one foot in front of the other and keep going. I tried not to agonize over the future, to remember our past well, to feel the pain of loss, and embrace the grief. Staying connected with my kids was a big part of it—they'd lost their mother. I was now the single parent of adult children."

I asked Mitch what sense he made of his and Sandie's stories, what sense he made of his second cancer following so quickly on the heels of his first, and of Sandie's cancer coming about the same time as his second diagnosis. And I asked if he ever asked himself why he lived and she died.

"It's puzzling," Mitch said. "There aren't answers. I have experienced suffering firsthand and live with the hope and trust that on some future day all things will be okay, but I don't know any answers. All we lived with the last year and a half of Sandie's life was cancer, first mine and then both of ours. I'd been teaching theology for almost two decades before all this happened, and my classes studied theodicy and all the wrong things there are to believe about why bad things happen to good people—or any people. I never asked, 'Why me?' You trust God but know all kinds of things happen along the way.

"I have often thought that if it was the case that if you had faith and prayed in the right way you'd get better, then everybody in the world would be Christian. But we serve a God who was the suffering, self-sacrificial servant. All of my study prepared me to know that those who follow God are not spared anything. God never promises to take away suffering. It's our witness and presence in the midst of suffering that shows our character, and I had lots of chances to think about what sort of person I wanted to be."

After ten months away from work, Mitch returned to Augustana in January 2020. "They were extremely gracious, but a number of things had changed," Mitch said. "I tried to come back, but in hindsight it was too early. It was actually good for me when the pandemic hit in March 2020, and everyone was sent home. I probably should have been home all along."

Mitch's experiences led him to make two significant changes. He began thinking hard about how he wanted to spend the rest of his professional career. Wanting to be more directly involved in people's lives, he asked several friends what they thought of him pursuing pastoral ministry. They were all affirming, and through connections with friends and former students, Mitch left Augustana and accepted a call to pastor a Lutheran church in East Saint Paul, Minnesota. "My suffering reoriented my perspective," he said. "My sense of life being short led me away from academia into pastoral ministry, where I'm dealing directly with suffering people. It's been fulfilling and meaningful. I feel very blessed to be able to do this."

In the course of his transition, Mitch made another change when he met a woman with whom he has begun a new relationship. "Sandie and I had talked about this," Mitch said, "because we knew there was a chance either one of us could die. We both believed we are created to be in relationships, and we gave each other our blessing to pursue a new relationship if one of us died. I'm sure that because I had come so close to dying, I have a heightened sense of life being short and was maybe more open to a new relationship than I might have been otherwise."

There's no guidebook that says when it's the right time to make major changes like moving, switching careers, or beginning a new relationship following a traumatic loss. In Mitch's case, the impact of the loss of his spouse is accentuated by his own cancer journey and his own brush with mortality. He repeated "life's too short" to me a number of times as we talked. His perspective obviously changed, and the church now held more appeal than the university. Life became too short to spend on institutional problems when there were people in the congregation with very pressing problems. And life became too short to spend alone. Yet as in most families, the adjustments to his new relationship affected his children.

"As any widow or widower knows," Mitch said, "while I can be in a new relationship, my kids won't ever have another mother, and that is hard."

The woman he began a relationship with also lives in the Twin Cities. Mitch has been cancer free for over four years, and now, over thirty years after earning his divinity degree, Mitch does the day-to-day work of a pastor. I asked him how he responds to people in his congregation who have cancer.

"I do what people did for us," he said. "I pray for healing and be as present as possible. Having survived, I am better able to be present with those who are suffering. I know there aren't things to say that will take the suffering away, but I do remember my own suffering as I share in theirs. Henri Nouwen's image of the wounded healer has long been a guiding metaphor, and I know it more intimately now. I'm much more empathetic as I minister to those who are hurting. And I remain hopeful: My trust in a God who suffered with creation gives me hope in a final redemption, whatever the immediate future holds."

～

Mitch and Sandie's story brought Cliff and Mary Anderson to mind. Cliff died from cancer in 2012, after being initially diagnosed in 2006. Like Mitch and Sandie, he'd also had a stem cell transplant as part of his treatment. Mary, who lives in Colorado Springs, has had a long career as a therapist. I first met her over four decades ago, on a spring day in 1980 when I was a few weeks away from college graduation and was talking to Cliff, then the Regional Director of Young Life in Michigan, about a staff position.

I had first met Cliff a couple of years earlier when I walked into my college dorm room following class one day. He was, rather incongruously, sitting in a corner eating a pineapple and talking to my roommate. He shook my hand and laughingly apologized for having sticky pineapple juice fingers, and I liked him right away.

On that day in 1980, when I was supposed to be talking to Cliff about job prospects, he instead asked me questions about how I was doing following my parents' separation. He knew them and knew they'd split up a few months earlier. I had a myriad of feelings about this, but no one had really asked me how I was doing before Cliff. We probably were together for ninety minutes and spent ten minutes on employment. The rest of the conversation was about the state of my heart and soul.

I did go to work for Cliff, and he spoiled me as a supervisor. He was a great encourager, wise, a tremendous listener, empathic, and a lot of fun. Working for Cliff meant spending time in his home, which let me get to know Mary better, along with their two sons. My time with the Anderson family increased exponentially in 1984, when Cliff introduced me to his niece Gretchen. We fell in love, and suddenly I saw a lot more of the Andersons. Cliff even officiated at our wedding in 1985. After Michigan, the Andersons moved to Colorado Springs. Mary established a private therapy practice there. Cliff served as Young Life's vice president for training. He also championed some of Young Life's most creative ministry forms, including ministry with young people in trouble with the legal system, young people with disabilities, and teen moms. He led Young Life's partnership with youth ministers in Germany, developed partnerships for Young Life with several seminaries, and taught classes for Young Life staff internationally. He had a profound impact on youth ministry around the world. Yet for all that, the end of his life was painful and difficult, and in some ways, Cliff and Mary's story mirrored Mitch and Sandie's.

I reached out to Mary and shared Mitch and Sandie's story with her. "This story is outside the range of normal," Mary said. "This is more loss than most people have to confront at one time. All of Mitch's losses are huge and horrendous, which puts this into the range of trauma."

We talked about trauma, and Mary echoed ideas that Dan
Rooks shared. She spoke of trauma's effects on the brain and body,
and how trauma takes up residence inside us.

"It's like a mosaic," Mary said. "You have different pieces of your
life, and this becomes a piece. As a therapist, my focus is on helping
people understand they are not going to get rid of it, and to see
that the goal is not to try to get over it. The goal is to learn how it
impacts you, how certain sensory things—something you hear or
see or smell—will trigger the body's memory of the trauma, and
to realize your first reaction is going to be a trauma reaction. What
you have to learn is how to manage it. That's why I like the phrase
'the stewardship of pain' so much. It's not that you get over trauma
or pretend it isn't there but instead the idea is to learn to become a
good steward of it. You let it instruct you. You let it make you more
sensitive and empathic with other people."

Mary used the analogy of loss as an enemy. "How do you suc-
cessfully deal with an enemy?" she asked. "You seek to understand
them. You look at them, learn about them, and understand who
they are and how they function. Then you can put them to rest.
But if you simply try to bury them alive before doing that work,
they will rise up and get you. That's why time alone following a loss
is so vital to healing. Mitch didn't have a choice—his own health
situation and then the pandemic dictated that he had to isolate
himself. But that was good. I just wanted to be alone after Cliff
died. I wanted to be alone with God. People would say, 'Why don't
you do this?' or 'Come be with these people so you won't be lonely.'
I wanted to be lonely. I wanted to step into the loss, see what it was
like, and see what God would do. That's something in Mitch's story
that reminded me of my story. Mitch's isolation was imposed, but I
think it helped him. My choice to be alone helped me."

∾

Many years ago, I had worked with Cliff at a Young Life camp and saw things that helped me understand how he handled his stem cell transplant. Even though he was the camp director, when we couldn't find him, he'd inevitably be in one of two places: either down in the shop, talking with the maintenance staff, or in the kitchen, working alongside the dishwashers. He never thought any person was more valuable than another, and his insatiable curiosity led him to ask all sorts of people—regardless of their station in life—questions about themselves. He always saw himself as a minister, so in his mind a prolonged hospital residency meant he had a new church. There were new people to get to know, and he befriended his nurses, doctors, and other members of the hospital staff. He learned their names, asked about their families, and listened intently to their stories. Although very ill, he insisted on getting out of bed each day and getting dressed and sitting in a chair. He would read, work, and talk.

"I would come to visit," Mary said, "and I would lie in the bed if it was empty. I was doing worse than he was. He made a project out of his recovery. He'd do things like count the ceiling tiles and say, 'I walked five tiles today, tomorrow I'm going for six,' like he was training for a marathon. He survived by moving forward. I'd just come in and know I wanted to lie in that bed. It was a long haul and very hard."

The stem cell transplant didn't buy Cliff a lot of extra time. Ultimately, the cancer prevailed, and the end of his life was difficult. Cancer spread throughout his body, including forming tumors on his spine and taking away the strength of his neck. He had to wear a cervical collar to hold his head up, and fell one day, which caused bleeding inside his brain. Surgery could repair the brain bleed, but his doctors were certain that simply positioning him on the operating table would snap his neck and kill him. He was conscious enough to understand that the doctors could no longer help him.

"He just laid in this bed," Mary said, "and no one would touch him because they were afraid that might break his neck. He wasn't moved, he wasn't touched, and we had to clean him up."

Hospice was called in and he was administered morphine to manage the pain. "At one point," Mary said, "he was asked if he wanted more morphine. They told him that if they gave him more, he would lose the ability to talk. Without hesitation he said, 'Give me more.' That's how bad the pain was. You might have thought Cliff, the talker, the relator, would want to hang on and talk more. But he chose to leave. There were no last words—no, 'Oh I love you and now I'm dying,' moments. It was ugly and awful and painful."

Mary had a moment at a window as Cliff died that parallels Mitch's experience as Sandie was dying. There were wildfires in the mountains around Colorado Springs where Cliff and Mary lived, and their neighborhood had been evacuated. Cliff's room was on the sixth floor of the hospital, and Mary could see the fires from that vantage point.

"If I looked out in one direction," Mary said, "I could see smoke, which I believed was coming from my house burning, and if I turned and looked in another direction, I could see my comatose husband dying. I was losing my home and my husband at the same time. I remember saying, 'Take it. Take the house. Take Cliff. But you're not getting me. I'm going to live. I'm not going down on that trauma ship.' There are times, like Mitch experienced, when you feel like you don't have anything left to give and you wonder how bad it can get."

For Mary, Cliff's death and the coincident wildfires became a picture of the difference between what happens to us and what happens inside of us. "We don't get to choose," she said, "what happens to us. But we do get to choose how we will respond. As I looked out that window, I thought of Deuteronomy 30:19 and those words about life and death being set before us. I chose life."

I asked Mary if she wondered why all of this had happened to her and Cliff, and what she made of Mitch's assertion that his theological training had prepared him for his loss.

"When Cliff was diagnosed," she said, "I don't remember us ever wondering 'why?' or wondering if God loved us. Those weren't questions we asked. Our question was 'what?', not 'why?' 'What now?' 'What did God have in store for us here?' I have always trusted that God loved me, even though I didn't like what was going on.

"With Mitch, I do believe his theological training made a big difference. His theology was the foundation of his resilience. What he believed about God, and what he believed about God's sacrificial love, mattered. His belief gives him hope, gives him resilience, and helps him be a good steward of a terrible experience.

"I believe in the power of our minds, and the power of intellect. We all know that our feelings just seem to come and go, but I maintain that what we know and believe makes a difference with our feelings. When I work with people who can't get out from under horrendous feelings, we do cognitive behavioral therapy. We look at what they think, and if we can change what they think, then their feelings will follow. You don't change your feelings by trying to change your feelings, but you can change your feelings by changing what you think. Feelings are created by what you think; by the story you tell yourself."

Indeed, the story we tell ourselves matters. After World War II, there were Japanese soldiers on isolated islands in the South Pacific who didn't know the war had ended. They held out not just for weeks or months, but for years! They were still in a war story when they should have been in a peace story.

"Mitch's thinking," Mary said, "was right on, and he was able to emerge and be resilient and hopeful because of his faith. We can never know what's next in our lives but can know the one in whom we have believed. We can know God and know that God loves us."

The questions that come with starting a new relationship after the loss of a spouse are further dimensions of how Mary's story parallels Mitch's. When is the time right to move in new directions, like changing career focus, or starting a new relationship? And how does a new relationship affect your children?

"I don't think Mitch made any changes too soon," Mary said, "because he did the work, spending time alone and going inside himself. It's not a matter of time, it's a matter of how you are responding. Mitch discovered what I discovered—when you're in that space where everything you've built your life on and depend on has been taken from you and cleared away, there is space for God in new and profound ways. Sometimes God may direct you in a new and different way. I'm not surprised Mitch made changes— he's open to the ways God is leading him."

But what about children?

"The loss of a parent is always hard on children," Mary said, "and Mitch is right when he points out that, though he can start a new relationship, his children won't have a new mother. When you have grown children, like Cliff and I did, and Mitch and Sandie did, a new spouse isn't really going to be a stepparent. The role isn't clearly defined and it's hard. It's scary for kids when parents remarry or start new relationships. The kids wonder if it means they're going to lose the surviving parent too. It takes a lot of reassurance and coming up with new ways to be together. As long as you're single, they know they've got you. When you remarry or move in that direction, they wonder if you are going to leave, too.

"Here's something often overlooked but important—one of the most important things people who want to help a friend after the loss of a spouse can do is reach out to their friend's children. Ask how they're doing. Be their friend. The lack of that adds to the grief."

Cliff and Mary were married for forty-six years. Mitch and Sandie were married for thirty-four years. I wondered if starting a new relationship might feel like you're being unfaithful to your "real" spouse.

"After Cliff died, I was single for five years," Mary said. "I fully embraced being single and learned a lot from the experience. Then the Lord brought Larry into my life. I never wondered, "What would Cliff think of this?" I just wondered what God was up to now. What would Cliff think? He'd want me to do anything I sincerely believed God was leading me to do. New relationships don't magically take away the pain of loss, and a new spouse doesn't take the place of someone you've lost. A new relationship is an addition, a new chapter in the story of your life. When I think of Cliff these days, it's not with some sort of guilt, but with sadness. I feel sad he missed retirement. We didn't get to do that part of our life together. He's missed the past decade; he's missed all that I've experienced. I feel bad and I feel sad about that."

∽

I keep thinking about a line from the beginning of the movie *Grand Canyon,* a line that not only describes a series of events in the movie but describes the stories of Mitch and Sandie and Cliff and Mary as well: "The world ain't supposed to work like this."

Sunrise on a beautiful Iowa August morning is supposed to bring gratitude and wonder, not the sense that God or the universe is playing a cruel trick. Defeating one kind of cancer is supposed to bring health, not open the door to another kind of cancer. A woman who is a beloved teacher, mother, and wife, who has helped and encouraged countless people, isn't supposed to die in her 50s. Wildfires, a product of extreme weather conditions, aren't supposed to devour homes. A man who is a vibrant minister, father, and husband, who also has helped and encouraged countless people, isn't supposed to die in his 60s.

How many of us have found ourselves, like Mitch, like Mary, standing motionless in front of a window, searching desperately for hope?

We may be shaking our heads, angrily thinking: The world ain't supposed to work like this!

There is a breach in the way things should be.

Yet somehow, as we stare out those open windows, the sun does rise. Mitch, Mary, Roger, Quentin, and so many others find the resilience and strength to go on. Now and then, they find, a mysterious grace shines through.

Mitch Kinsinger is Senior Pastor of Arlington Hills Lutheran Church in St. Paul, Minnesota. www.AHLC-STP.org

Mary Anderson is a therapist based in Colorado Springs, Colorado. She holds a bachelor's degree from Whitworth University and a master's in social work from the University of Chicago.

6

The Long Goodbye

"The betrayals of body and mind that threaten to erase our character and memory remain among our most awful tortures."
Public health expert Atul Gawande

"Dealing faithfully with dementia is a new frontier. … Can we become the guardians of someone's personhood when they can no longer hold it for themselves? That's a term I like for caretakers: they are guardians of someone's personhood."
Theologian Suzanne McDonald

Sometime around my mother's 75th birthday, my brother took her out for lunch. When they were in the car, she asked where they were going.

"Charley Brown's," he said. It was a favorite of theirs, a restaurant they visited often.

"Whoever heard of a place called Charley Brown's?" she said. "What sort of a name for a restaurant is that?"

That was the first clue. Others followed.

My brothers, our spouses, and our children gathered on both my mother's and father's 75th birthdays. The celebration for my father took place in Michigan, the one for my mother took place in Southern California. On those occasions, my siblings and I wrote tributes to each parent and read them aloud. A friend of mine suggested this: Why wait until a funeral to say the things you should say to each other? I'm glad we did them, especially glad considering the memory loss my mother was facing. Thankfully, she was all there when we gathered for her birthday and took in everything we said. But in a few months, lots of information had slipped from her brain.

A fog descended.

My parents divorced at midlife; my mom was 47 when they separated. Twenty-eight years later, she was living across the country with my stepfather, Chuck, when she started the long, slow, sad goodbye of Alzheimer's disease. She lived for six years after the diagnosis, and the first five years were not terrible. My mother was one of those people who was naturally nice and kind, and Alzheimer's did not change that aspect of her personality. She remained happy and upbeat, and never wandered away from home the way some memory-loss patients do. She had always been anxious when negotiating the Southern California freeway system, so giving up driving was a relief, not a burden. And there was this: Her divorce had been the most painful experience of her life. It was a sort of grace to have that pain erased. As bad as Alzheimer's is—and it is awful—it sometimes can be a blessing not to remember the worst things that have happened to you.

Chuck took care of her as long as he could, probably even a little longer than he should have, but he told me that being her caretaker gave his life meaning and purpose. Chuck was never much of a churchgoer, but my mother had, in her kind and gentle way (which others might call Midwestern passive-aggressive), more or less forced him to attend worship regularly with her over the years. Then, as Chuck took this new responsibility on, he joined an early morning Bible study with some of the men from their church that gave him much needed support and nourishment for the journey.

Because she didn't wander, he had the freedom to leave their home, a freedom many caretakers of those with dementia do not have.

As her memory faded, her capacity for delight was endless. A single accomplishment by one of her grandchildren could make her happy thirty times in the same evening. "You speak French? And German? That's wonderful!" "You got a job working with computers? That's great!"

As time passed, she forgot who we were, and we'd look at photo albums together and tell her the stories of her life. "Here's a picture of you taking care of your grandson Jesse. You came out to Michigan to help us after he was born."

"I did? Well, I must have been happy to do that."

"I believe it made you very happy."

"I'm sure it did." It made her happy to think that she had been happy.

Even after she'd forgotten our names, she still remembered the Lord's Prayer and other liturgical elements from church. Like many Alzheimer's patients, she remembered music. One afternoon we were visiting, and I said, "Mom, do you remember this?" and started singing "Amazing Grace." She joined in immediately. My wife, Gretchen, came in on the second verse, and then Chuck joined on the third, and by the time we got to "When we've been there ten thousand years," my brother, who lived close to her in California, also joined in from across the room. Tears formed in our eyes as we had this rare moment of connection. It was a sacred, holy moment amid a sea of forgetfulness. After a minute, my brother, being my brother, couldn't help but see what would happen if he sang the first line of "Moon River," another of her old favorites, and of course she joined in. Maybe not as holy as "Amazing Grace," but a moment of connection, nonetheless.

One night I called to check in and after a few minutes on the phone she asked me when I had become her son.

"On the day I was born," I said. "You gave birth to me."

"Well, I'm sure I did if you say so. But where do you live now?"

"I live in Michigan," I said, "where you used to live. This is where I've lived pretty much my whole life."

"I live out here," she said. "A man named Chuck has been kind enough to give me a room to stay in."

"That's your home," I said. "Chuck is your husband."

She laughed and said, "He's not my husband."

"Yes, he is," I said.

Then I heard her say to Chuck, "He thinks you're my husband."

I could hear Chuck say from across the room, "That's what I've been trying to tell you."

On one of our last visits, when she was still at home, she and Chuck came over to our hotel to have breakfast with Gretchen and me. Halfway through breakfast, I smelled something off, and saw urine dripping down my mother's chair. We did the best we could to get things cleaned up, but how wrong is that? I felt like crying. The loss of dignity is an outrage, yet she wasn't even aware of it.

Alzheimer's is a thief; it took everything it could from her. Despite Chuck's heroic efforts, she eventually required a care facility. The fog got worse and worse. The last few months of her life involved much suffering. The ease of the early stages was long gone, and I saw firsthand that Alzheimer's is a terrible way to die. I last visited her two weeks before her death. It happened to be my 55th birthday, which wound up being one of the saddest days of my life. As I entered the open area of the care facility, I saw someone slumped in a wheelchair, a person in such bad shape that I averted my eyes. I glanced again and realized that person was my mother. She hadn't known who I was for years, so I didn't have high expectations for the day, but I was devastated by how much worse she had become. She had changed dramatically: she'd lost the ability to speak and lost the ability to hold her head up. She had aged decades in the few months since I had last seen her. She looked, for the first time in her life, old. Her eyes were unfocused, gazing and searching, but not really seeing.

I told her who I was and put my hand on her forearm and gave a little squeeze.

She said, "Ow."

It would be the last word I ever heard her speak.

This is how life ends for many of us. We imagine our lives as wonderful stories that are playing out like epic novels or movies. In the rare moments when we imagine our deaths, they are never like this. We see ourselves lying in bed, with our family members gathered close, saying meaningful things, and resolving all the unresolved tensions of our relationships. Or we see ourselves dying "perfect" deaths, painlessly and in our sleep at age 100. We don't imagine spending weeks or months or years in care facilities tended by strangers. We don't imagine dying with no knowledge of who our family is, incontinent, unable to speak, or even hold up one's head.

On that last day, I sought my own resolution with my mother. I was certain this was the last time I would see her in this lifetime. I'd gone out for lunch with my brother and when I came back, the staff of the care facility had put my mom to bed. I sat with her for a while longer until it was time to head to the airport. I then knelt beside her and told her that I loved her, told her she'd been a great mother, and told her that I was glad that out of all the people in the world she was my mother. I then choked up as I said, "Mom, I think you've done all you're supposed to do here. I want you to know it's okay with me if you die now. I don't want you to hold on for my sake or the sake of any of us. Please don't try to stay alive on our account. I want you to go be with Jesus, you're going to have a much better, happier life in the presence of Jesus." I had mixed feelings as I said those things, simultaneously feeling it was the right thing to say and yet also feeling like a rat because I'd just said, "It's okay with me if you die now."

Both loving son and betraying son, I put my hand on her head and said, "Mom, I want to pray." The first words out of my mouth came as a surprise to me. I said, "Lord, forgive us our sins."

Why would I say that? I have puzzled over those words for a long time. Years later, I would learn from a hospice chaplain that there are four basic questions as people face death: Do I love you? Do you love me? Do I forgive you? Do you forgive me?

After driving back to the airport that day, I tried to capture some of the feelings behind my unexpected prayer for forgiveness in a poem:

**After Seeing an Ant-Covered Sack Lunch
Some Kid Had Left Next to the Creek**

Initial revulsion followed by slow realization—
There was something familiar about that brown bag—
So he kicked it and watched the ants scurry.

And recognized the fold of the napkin inside.
He had sat in the lunchroom mystified,
Steaming in self-pity.

His older brothers had lunches,
Why would she make him go hungry?
But now there was overwhelming evidence,

Evidence that spoke to his carelessness,

Evidence that he would shamefully watch decompose over the coming weeks,

A signpost in a lifetime of disconnection.

Many years later he makes her a sandwich,

And slowly folds a napkin as a small act of atonement

During the long years of her decomposition.

As I wrote the poem, I was thinking about a day many years ago that I'd gotten to school without my lunch and had sat stewing in the lunchroom, angry at my mother for forgetting me. Of course, it was me who was the forgetful one, as I discovered when I saw what was supposed to be my lunch, now covered with ants. I must have set my lunch down to throw some rocks into the creek when I cut through the woods behind our house on my way to school. That lunch bag stayed where it was for a long time, and I'd see it every day, bearing silent and shameful testimony to my carelessness. Of course, I said to myself as I drove up the freeway to the airport, I was just a kid and kids do careless stuff like that all the time. I could forgive myself for that. But could I forgive myself for how angry I'd been at her? What was up with that?

I also thought about my ninth birthday. My mom had found a recipe for a cake made with Heath bars, an English candy bar filled with toffee. That would have been fine except I *hated* toffee (it always made me feel like my teeth were in danger of breaking) and, as a result, hated Heath bars. I still don't like them. I have a brother, though, who is a Heath bar fanatic. My mom had gotten this mixed up. Being nine years old, I lacked the maturity to point this out in any sort of reasonable way. My mom brought out the Heath bar birthday cake and I immediately concluded this was some sort of cruel joke she was playing on me and started crying.

"I hate you," I screamed as I slammed the door to my bedroom and laid down on my bed to wallow in self-pity.

And I thought about my parents' divorce. There's been plenty of forgiveness and healing and goodness since then, but at the time it was terribly painful. They'd both been very active in our church, serving as elders and singing in the choir. Our house at times seemed like an extension of the church—kids from the youth group were always around and our family's identity was tied closely to our church. When my dad divorced my mom, he also divorced our church. He never went back and didn't stay connected to the friends he had there. It was a seismic change in our lives. But then my mother reconnected with Chuck. They'd known each other in high school, and had dated before my parents were married. She married Chuck two years after my dad left and then she moved from Michigan to California. As a result, she'd see me, my wife, and our kids once or maybe twice a year. My kids loved having a California grandmother who lived close to Disneyland. I was always aware of the distance and the loss of regular contact, knowing whenever we were together it wouldn't be long until we had to say goodbye.

A friend said once that the experience of being human breaks every heart. As a result, all we have to give each other are pieces of our broken hearts, and they are never enough. There is much wisdom in his words. We want to be known and loved completely, but never are. We long to love our family members fully but never do. Whatever we do, it is never enough. We never are loved enough. We never love enough. We are imperfect lovers, needy people, never fully satisfied, never fully known, always wanting and needing more than those around us can give.

And so, at my dying mother's bedside, I surprised myself by praying, "Forgive us our sins."

We do the best we can, but it is never enough. I understand that generational conflict and trauma in many families far outweighs ours. My family story is not marked by abuse or negligence or abandonment. I suppose I was asking more for forgiveness for sins of omission rather than commission. My mom never talked to me about my father and the pain of her divorce. She never spoke meaningfully about her marriage to Chuck. And although she was their primary caregiver, she bore the decline and eventual deaths of her parents silently. I felt I had her approval and blessing, but she never asked many questions about my life or work. We didn't ever talk in depth about what mattered most.

At her bedside, I prayed, "Forgive us our sins," not just for the thoughtless and hurtful things we'd said and done over the years, but more than that for never being all we could be to each other, for never loving each other fully or completely.

All we have to give each other are the pieces of our broken hearts and they are never enough.

A few months after my mother's death, I tried to express some of this in a poem formatted as if my words were flowing into a rectangular container, hoping somehow it could hold all my mixed feelings.

Memory

I could handle the questions repeated endlessly like we were in Groundhog Day: Who are you? Where do you live now? When did you become my son? You told me a man had been kind enough to give you a room in his house and when I said that man was your husband you laughed and laughed. You kept your good nature and smile as your world was reduced—first to the apartment, then a room, then just a chair. In a rare moment of clarity, you looked around and said, "So this is the way it's going to be." No, it wasn't. It got worse. Confusion yielded to terror. Words became moans. Your head was a weight too heavy to bear, your skin was on fire, your muscles rigid, your eyes endlessly searched for something, anything familiar. You forgot to eat, then breathe. There was no point to any of this. You just suffered. For senseless days, weeks, months. Who are you? I wondered. Where do you live now? When did you become my mother? Like an overdue guest, death finally arrived, and at your funeral people said the images of suffering would fade and I would be left with positive memories. But what I'm left with, besides the god-awful fear that this will someday happen to me, is the sight of you slumped in that wheelchair, incoherent, uncomprehending, my mother yet not my mother in any way I want to believe. You couldn't remember, I can't forget. What is memory, anyway? A blessing? ... A curse?

The week I was writing this chapter, Gretchen and I shared dessert with some long-time friends, a couple we've known for forty years. The husband and I have had some fun adventures together. Once, we traveled to the Baseball Hall of Fame and talked our way into the basement, where countless treasures are stored, because we wanted to meet the curator. On another occasion, we took in the first night game at Wrigley Field. I had helped perform the wedding of one of their children, and when our youngest child was born, the wife, who worked as an obstetrics nurse, had come into the hospital on her night off to help Gretchen through the delivery. Over dessert the husband explained that his wife had recently been diagnosed with Alzheimer's disease.

Our hearts broke.

Then he told about her getting lost on multiple occasions, both driving and walking away from their house. Through this entire description, she sat with us at the table. At length, she said, "Please don't pity me."

I'm sure she meant pity in the sense of turning a friend into an object, but we couldn't help being filled with sorrow. The purpose of this meeting over dessert was not only to let us know what was going on, but to invite us in to be a part of a circle of people who would walk with them in the months and years ahead. It was moving and heartbreaking—and courageous and wise. I thought: They know they need help.

But I couldn't help feeling rage on top of compassion. As Atul Gawande wrote in *Being Mortal*, "The betrayals of body and mind that threaten to erase our character and memory remain among our most awful tortures. The battle of being mortal is the battle to maintain the integrity of one's life—to avoid becoming so diminished or dissipated or subjugated that who you are becomes disconnected from who you were or who you want to be."

Alzheimer's is wrong. It destroys the integrity of life and it is torture. I hate it.

～

I was eager to talk this over with Suzanne McDonald. A native of Australia, Suzanne is a dynamo, full of life and verve, and liable at any moment to call you "mate" or say she's "chuffed" (which turns out to be a good thing). If life was a *Star Wars* movie, some Yoda-like sage would say, "The Force is strong in this one." She's brilliant—after earning an undergraduate degree at the University of Western Australia in Perth, she went to the United Kingdom and earned a master's degree in English literature from Oxford, a master's degree in theology from Cambridge, and a Ph.D. in theology from St. Andrews. She is an ordained minister in the Christian Reformed Church and professor of systematic and historical theology at Western Theological Seminary. On top of all that, she has a vast knowledge of dementia.

In the 1990s, before pursuing her graduate degrees in theology and her calling in ministry, Suzanne worked for the Red Cross in Australia. Her supervisor and his wife became good friends. The wife was diagnosed with early-onset dementia (before age 65), which can progress more quickly than other kinds of dementia, and, in her case, it was eighteen months from diagnosis to death. Suzanne's friend went from being a gentle, hospitable, loving woman to someone terrified of everything. She became violent—even going after her husband with a kitchen knife at one point. This had a huge impact on Suzanne, and she began exploring how the experience of dementia might fit into the world of faith and theology. She not only read everything she could on dementia, she also worked in a dementia ward as part of her ministry training. Over the past few decades, Suzanne has presented dozens of seminars on dealing faithfully with dementia in churches and other settings.

She began our conversation by explaining that dementia is an umbrella term that includes multiple conditions with a wide range of symptoms and causes. Different forms of dementia affect different parts of the brain and sometimes they are associated with diseases like Huntington's and Parkinson's. Generally, dementia's warning signs include severe deterioration of recent memory, an inability to hold up one's end of a conversation, losing track of appointments and money, and difficulty doing regular tasks. Often as the disease progresses, the person's personality may change dramatically. Because of the varieties of dementia, there are different prognoses and life expectancies.

Alzheimer's is the most common form of dementia, and at any given time affects around 6 million people in the United States, and 44 million worldwide. I knew that Alzheimer's was named for the doctor who first identified the disease early in the past century, and wondered if dementia has always been with us or if this is something that's developed in the past century or so.

"It's more prevalent now," Suzanne said, "because people are living longer. But I'm a 17th century literature nerd when I'm not doing my theology stuff, and you'll find in diaries and other places people describing what we now know as Alzheimer's. Even though the average age of death was lower then, some people still lived into their 70s and 80s and even 90s, so you do get people describing symptoms that are not general aging. But it's more prevalent now, and the expectation is that it will increase exponentially as Baby Boomers age. No one knows what causes Alzheimer's, but I suspect the chemical cocktail of industrialization may have much to do with it. Sometimes when dementia is linked to another disease we know its cause, but by and large we don't know what causes the various types of dementia, or why some people get it and others don't, or how to prevent it.

"To some degree, everyone is terrified of it. Every time you have a memory blip you wonder if this is the start of Alzheimer's or dementia. But everyone has memory lapses, that's a normal part of aging. Alzheimer's and dementia are not normal parts of aging. It's not something people should expect will happen to them. Yes, you are more likely to get it when you are over 75, but that doesn't mean you will get it if you are over 75. It's a disease, not a regular part of aging."

~

The primary image Suzanne uses for constructing a theology of dementia is Holy Saturday, the often-overlooked day that lies between Good Friday and Easter Sunday.

"We seem to want to jump," Suzanne said, "straight from Good Friday to Resurrection Sunday. We don't want to dwell in the pain and aftermath of Good Friday. We push people too quickly from a space where lament and protest are appropriate reactions to 'Oh, everything's okay because of Jesus somehow.' That says more about our discomfort with pain and lament than anything else. The Psalms give us language for this and permission to lament and protest. Holy Saturday provides space in the story, space in the narrative, to hold our lament and protest and hurt and pain and confusion.

"Yes, we know what happens on Easter Sunday, but can we also imagine what it must have been like for those first disciples on that first Holy Saturday? What Jesus said about rising from the dead was completely gone from their minds. As far as they were concerned, the horrendous event on Good Friday had instantiated the new normal for the rest of their lives. It was bleak. The glimpses we get of them processing that loss, the glimpses of what it must have felt like, are similar to what it's like to walk the dementia road.

"Jesus had lost his identity for the disciples. Following his death, and before the resurrection, he was no longer who they thought he was. Look at what's said on the road to Emmaus: 'We had hoped he was the one to restore Israel.' But now? With Jesus losing his identity, or seeming to for the disciples, the disciples also lose their identities. They had identified themselves as the followers of Jesus, they had dedicated their lives to him. Now when his identity seems to be lost, their identity disintegrates along with his. They lock themselves into the Upper Room, absolutely terrified that what had happened to Jesus was going to happen to them. We can easily imagine they felt guilt, abandonment, resentment, and frustration at their inability to set anything right. They'd given their whole lives to Jesus and had nothing to show for it. It had all disintegrated. They felt hopeless.

"Dementia feels hopeless. In many ways it is hopeless. There's no cure. There are treatments that might slow it down, but nothing is going to change. It's only going to get worse. The identity of your loved one is falling apart right before your eyes. If you're a caregiver, your identity is going to be lost to the person with dementia. There will come a time when someone you love deeply no longer recognizes you. And to the rest of the world, your new identity is going to be as a dementia person's caregiver. Whatever else you might be, whatever else you might have been, you're now a person who cares for someone with dementia. There are a lot of identity issues at play. And there's fear. Fear that it will happen to you also. Fear of all the losses that are coming. Dementia is like an extended Holy Saturday.

"When I speak about dealing faithfully with dementia, I also ask people to remember that Holy Saturday was the Jewish Sabbath day. Those first disciples were gathered in fear, but they kept the Sabbath. No matter what else they were feeling—including being resentful and confused—they were doggedly faithful and kept the Sabbath. So too for the people caring for someone with dementia. Even after their emotions are depleted, even when they don't feel strong love anymore, they keep caring. They may be volcanically angry, but like the first disciples, they are doggedly faithful. Even when you can't understand and you can't hold everything together, the faithful Sabbath-keeping aspect of Holy Saturday is a space that holds you.

"There is another Sabbath aspect of Holy Saturday: The rest of us need to find ways to give those caregivers a Sabbath. We need to find ways to enable them to have something of the fullness of life and to experience having more to their lives than simply being someone who cares for a person with dementia.

"There are many facets to Holy Saturday that resonate with the dementia journey. Here's one more: There's a tension between the need to honor the person with dementia, to still see them as a person made in the image of God, and the language we use like, 'He's gone,' or 'She's no longer there.' It is simultaneously true that the person with dementia still bears the image of God and yet they are also disintegrating. Holy Saturday strikes that balance. You're between two poles. We affirm that God is faithful and remembers, but you're living a horrific reality. What hope you have will only be realized when the person with dementia beholds God face to face and they know as they are known and are fully redeemed. But that feels awfully distant much of the time."

~

When I asked what was typical in my story, Suzanne cautioned about using the word "typical."

"There's no such thing as typical," she said. "Every person is unique. It's not helpful to expect dementia to progress in a linear fashion or think there are steps to it. Everybody is different, and every case is a 'special case.'" Having said that, she did say there were elements of my story that many others walking the dementia road would identify with.

"You made the observation," Suzanne said, "that perhaps your stepfather took care of your mother longer than he should have. This is one of the most fraught conversations any family will have. How do you honor your 'in sickness and in health' wedding vows and yet also acknowledge the time has come when the best care is more than you can offer? This is a crunch point in almost every dementia journey. And the loss of dignity is surely a part of every dementia story. This may manifest in several ways, but as you reported, it's often experienced in a loss of our most elemental bodily functions. The heartbreak of your birthday is also something many will identify with—not only that she didn't recognize you, but you didn't initially recognize her.

"Positively, the connection through music is something many experience. I'm grateful you included 'Moon River', because we often want to spiritualize these things. We ought to give people with dementia the gift of all kinds of music we know they've enjoyed. In the Christian context we focus on hymns, and wind up choosing sad hymns. A friend of mine once said that every time he went into a dementia ward and heard singing it sounded like a rehearsal for everyone's funeral. Music is a wonderful way to connect, but sing some happy hymns, please.

"Something that I found heartening in your story is that Chuck found support from the other guys at church. Too often that is not the case. I hear many stories that are the opposite. It gets too hard and the church cannot sustain walking alongside folks in this extended struggle. Their care fades away. Churches are often very good at short-term projects, like bringing meals when a baby is born, but walking alongside for the long haul is a challenge. Dementia is often a long journey—this could last a decade or more."

I asked what's redemptive about dementia and Suzanne paused and thought.

"The sad truth is there's not much redemptive in dementia. It robs someone of the fullness of who they are. It is, as you noted, a thief, and it robs the rest of us of our experience of the person too. Yet along the way there are little shafts of light that shine through. There are small mercies, moments of unexpected joy and delight. As you noted, the forgetting of painful memories can be a blessing. Or maybe someone who has forgotten their spouse's name will remember it out of the blue one day. That can be a blessing. Yet those moments are often bittersweet because they come as part of a wider story of pain. Just mentioning redemption makes me wary of the pious moves we sometimes make. We're uncomfortable with the horror of what is unfolding so we try to make it into something it's not.

"The first move is to simply own the reality of what's happening. That's the Holy Saturday move. It's not from cross to resurrection but from cross to tomb. God gave us this day in the middle of the story, a day to acknowledge pain and confusion and awfulness and bleakness. Sometimes we just need to acknowledge that and stick with it and dwell in that space without talking about redemption or resurrection. But after giving people space for that first move, the second is to give thanks for what I sometimes call the small 'resurrection moments' that can come in the midst of dementia—those shafts of light, those moments of recognition—which are an anticipation now of the fullness of life and identity that will eventually be theirs when they behold the Lord face to face and know as they are known.

"Dealing faithfully with dementia is a new frontier. Both Ronald Reagan and Margaret Thatcher ended up having dementia, but their families were not very open about it. Those were lost opportunities. It often takes a famous person or two to go public with their struggle for the wider society to become more knowledgeable and accepting. When I talk about this at churches, the audience is typically older, so I always mention how Betty Ford was open about both addiction and breast cancer. Recently, I'm grateful for the way Glen Campbell's family was open with his story and I'm grateful for *I'll Be Me*, the documentary about him. Glen Campbell could still do all this amazing stuff with his guitar while his family was having a very difficult time with him. They struggled with the decision of when to put him into a care facility—he was too strong for them, he'd be obstreperous and violent. After they put him in care his wife received death threats from his fans—that shows how much work we still need to do."

As I talked with Suzanne, I thought of one of my favorite maxims: "When you're through learning, you're through." Yet when I think about this saying in the light of dementia, I'm troubled. What is learning other than the ability to remember? Yet it's futile to correct someone with dementia or try to teach them something. They aren't going to remember what you say, so you're just wasting your breath. I asked Suzanne about the relationship of personhood to memory.

"So many of our interactions," Suzanne said, "are based on short-term memory. Or, technically, shorter-term memory, since in the proper medical sense short-term memory is only the past couple of seconds. Much of what we think of as personhood is related to shorter-term memory. It's vitally important to realize there is more to personhood than memory. If all we focus on is memory, we are going to struggle to see personhood in someone in the depths of dementia.

"It's also important to note there are different kinds of memory. We've talked about how people with dementia may retain music—that's connected to something called procedural memory. It lasts the longest. You'll remember how to do things—how to ride a bike or play an instrument. And there's emotional memory, a term you don't hear often. Smells can be connected with emotional memory. For example, every time you smell the kind of cigar your dad smoked—whew, off you go. In dementia, emotional memory can be triggered by other senses: smell, taste, and so on. The person with dementia may not be able to articulate what it is they're remembering, but you can tell something is going on.

"As we think of someone's personhood and how to walk well with someone with dementia, we should ask how we can tap into these other types of memory. Can we become the guardians of someone's personhood when they can no longer hold it for themselves? That's a term I like for caretakers: They are guardians of someone's personhood."

The question really is, "What makes you—*you?*" Certainly, there must be more than just the ability to remember that defines our personhood.

"You cannot be who you are without a network of people," Suzanne said, "the web of relationships that you are in. And personhood is not just inward things; it's the way your hair is done, your favorite clothes, the way you do your nails, the aftershave you use—all of these physical things, these nonmemory things, go into making someone who they are, into the fullness of their personhood. That's significant as we hold onto the sense of someone's personhood amid the ravages of this disease.

"I heard a story about a man who had been put into a care home and kept fussing with his wrists and hands, almost wringing his hands constantly. It's common for people with dementia to be fidgety, so the people at the care home didn't think much about it. But when a friend came to visit, he said that his friend never considered himself fully dressed unless he had his cufflinks in. The man with dementia wasn't fidgeting as much as communicating that he wanted his cufflinks. His friend got them for him. That's what it means to be a guardian of someone's personhood.

"How can we see and honor someone's personhood in ways that aren't memory dependent? Those who see reason as our greatest gift and what makes us in the image of God have a real problem here. The idea that reason makes us close to God isn't biblical. The heart of the image of God is relationship; primarily God's relationship with us. We can be guardians of someone's personhood, but God is the guarantor. Even if your memory goes, you don't lose your personhood. Romans 8 says that nothing in life or death, which certainly includes dementia, can separate us from the love of God in Christ. The lens of dementia also sheds light on a mysterious verse, Colossians 3:3: that your life is hidden with Christ in God. I think this means our personhood is kept even when we cannot keep it for ourselves. Being made in the image of God is a statement about God's relationship with us. This takes us many steps toward seeing someone whose memory is gone as a person still worthy of respect and love and honor. This allows us to think wider about how to sustain someone's personhood when they cannot do it themselves."

~

But what then are we to make of the Bible's many passages about memory? The Bible is full of commands to remember, from remembering that God brought Israel out of slavery in Egypt to Jesus saying, "Do this in remembrance of me." Remembering isn't a minor theme of the Bible, it's a major theme, mentioned repeatedly.

"This is one of those points," Suzanne said, "where we have to recognize that dementia puts huge question marks on so many of the ways we regularly think of faith and how it is expressed and how we live it. One of the keys is to realize that all these imperatives in the Bible are communal. My personal intellectual recall is important, but remembering happens in community, in the people of God. We remember with and for each other and are collectively taken up into the story. Everyone, not just those with dementia, forgets parts of the story. We can go days at a time without giving God a second thought. Do we always act in ways that are consistent with our identity as people in this story? No, we do not! If grace is there for us, it's there in the situation of dementia too. Communal remembering is a large part of worship, and we do see that elements of worship tend to stick with those with dementia. Hymns stick. The Lord's Prayer sticks. People in highly liturgical traditions—Roman Catholics and Episcopalians and Anglicans— find that the rhythms and movements of liturgy are etched deep into the brain and people with dementia in those traditions are standing and sitting and kneeling at all the right times and saying all the right words. Worship can hold people with dementia in the story when they can't fully hold themselves. The community does that for them.

"A parallel can be made with infant baptism—before that baby knows the first thing about who God is or what God has done in Christ, that baby is enfolded by God into the covenant community, the community of the story. This happens also at the other end of life, with people with dementia. When the person with dementia can no longer remember for themselves, they are still held in the covenant faithfulness of God. What matters most is not our remembering, it's God's remembering. This is a golden thread running throughout the scriptures. God will never forget God's people. Look at Isaiah 49:15: Can a nursing mother forget her child? Even if she could, God says, I will never forget. You are engraved on the palms of my hands.

"God's memory in scripture is not just a noun but an active verb. When God remembers, things happen. When he remembers his people in Egypt, the Exodus happens. Look at what it says about God's memory in those two great songs that begin Luke's Gospel, the Magnificat, and the song of Zechariah: God has remembered his mercy, God has remembered his covenant and sent the Messiah. God's redemptive remembering makes things happen. This is a reminder for us that even in the midst of dementia, where there is no human hope for a cure, there is the assurance I mentioned earlier that we cannot lose our personhood. It is kept for us in God, and God is present and at work in the situation of dementia, and that his redeeming work encompasses even the bleakest aspects of this awful disease.

"I've had people in tears in front of me wondering if their parent with dementia has lost their faith and lost their salvation because of the blasphemous things dementia is making their parent say. But God does not hold that against them. God keeps them and remembers who they are. Jesus Christ will carry them through this."

I have felt that Holy Saturday tension, not only during my mother's dementia journey, but in other parts of my life. As I mentioned earlier, my interest in the stewardship of pain goes back to the night of Gretchen's stroke in 1985. I stepped onto an elevator that night with a woman who identified herself as the supervisor of nursing at the hospital.

Without an introduction, she knew who I was and what was happening. She expressed her sadness that Gretchen was in the hospital and then said, "You may not believe it, but this too shall pass." There was deep kindness and compassion in her voice.

It was hard to believe, but it also felt like a glimmer of light in the darkness.

Holy Saturday does eventually give way to Easter Sunday. Jesus didn't stay in the tomb forever. Those stuck in the fog of dementia don't stay there forever. Being a good steward along the dementia road means faithfully living in the tension of the in-between time, confident of the reality that not even dementia can separate us from the love of God, but also willing to name the horrific reality of the darkness surrounding us.

We may not believe it, but this too shall pass.

Suzanne McDonald is Professor of Systematic and Historical Theology at Western Theological Seminary. www.WesternSem.edu/faculty/ mcdonald

7

How Do We Hold Our Pain?

"Trauma is not just an event that took place sometime in the past; it is also the imprint left by that experience on mind, brain, and body."
Psychologist Bessel van der Kolk

"As we engage and truthfully tell our stories, we become more integrated and pull away the layers so we may become a whole person, able to hold pain and joy together, able to hold complexity and embrace oneness."
Psychologist Chuck DeGroat

A friend and I were talking the other day about his relationship with his father, who can be quite materialistic and narcissistic. The son is more level-headed and rational. Surprisingly, they have a decent relationship, which made me curious because a lot of people have a hard time with the father. But the son maintains a positive relationship.

How is that possible? How does the son put up with his father's excesses and irrationality?

The son told me, "I just remember that my dad was traumatized when he was a child. Some part of his development got stuck there.

There are parts of my dad that are childish. I try to steer clear of those parts whenever I can."

I had forgotten, but remembered when the son mentioned it, that many years ago I had heard stories about his father's childhood. This man's father, my friend's grandfather, had been domineering and manipulative and emotionally abusive to his wife and son and daughter. One day, when my friend's father was a child of 12, he came home from school and found his mother had killed herself in the family garage. Unsure what to do, the boy called his father at work. The father exploded, saying that the boy knew better than to disturb him at the office. The boy went outside, intercepted his younger sister on her way home from school, and kept her away from the garage until the father came home.

That evening, after the police and emergency personnel were gone, the father went into a rage again, angry that he had been forced to deal with this mess, angry that his son had not taken care of it.

It's terrible enough that his mother committed suicide in the family garage. The abuse on top of that adds a layer of traumatic complexity. It's accurate to say the boy was traumatized by this event. But it's more than that. He lived with his abusive father before and after his mother's suicide. Nobody should face that, and my heart breaks for him.

But here's the problem: He isn't that little boy anymore. The coping behaviors that helped him survive as a child aren't needed as an adult, but those behaviors are hard-wired into him. Somehow parts of him are stuck in that trauma. It's difficult now that the adult has parts of his personality that behave as if he was a child.

How does that happen? How is it that some of us get stuck in our pain?

This is some of the terrain Frederick Buechner writes about in his essay "Adolescence and the Stewardship of Pain." He identifies two unhealthy ways we cope with pain. The first is to ignore it or pretend it doesn't exist, to take the route of the stoic and the stiff upper lip, which he calls burying pain. The alternative is to become trapped in your pain, the route of Charles Dickens' character Miss Havisham in *Great Expectations*, who was jilted by her intended husband and ever after sits in a darkened room in a wedding dress that is turning to rags upon her while her uneaten wedding cake molders.

I decided to take a detour—instead of going in depth into one story, I wanted some help understanding why we process pain so differently. The stories in this book are about people who have taken pain into their being. Yet we all know others who don't seem able to process their pain at all. Some people seem controlled by their pain, become their pain, while others deny its existence.

I turned to Dr. Chuck DeGroat for help navigating this. Chuck has a Ph.D. in psychology, teaches pastoral care and counseling at Western Theological Seminary, maintains a private counseling practice, and is the author of several books, including *When Narcissism Comes to Church* (2020), *Wholeheartedness: Busyness, Exhaustion, and Healing the Divided Self* (2016), and *Toughest People to Love: How to Understand, Lead, and Love the Difficult People in Your Life—Including Yourself* (2014). Each of Chuck's books relates mental health challenges to life in the church. He has a unique ability to apply scientific knowledge and psychological insights to ordinary life and describe things in understandable language.

When I told Chuck the story of my friend's father, the traumatized boy who is now a difficult adult, he said, "It's helpful that your friend used the word 'parts.' Your friend said, 'Parts of my father are childish.' I appreciate that language because it's become a very helpful way to name how we hold pain. We hold it in a part of our self. Our brains work to protect us—they are amazing organs focused on survival. At any moment we are being exposed to millions of bits of data that our brains are subconsciously processing. We explicitly process much less, but our brains are constantly organizing, sorting, and compartmentalizing data all the time. Our brains take in pain, and by compartmentalizing pain, our brains allow us to survive monumental pain. It's important to remember that our varied responses to pain are ways our brains are helping us survive.

"There are several different schools of thought that have named the different parts or subpersonalities or alter egos that we have. One approach that's been helpful to me is the Internal Family Systems model, which was developed by Richard Schwartz. Schwartz was trained in family systems, and applied the understanding of what happens in external systems to internal systems.

"There's no question our personalities are shaped by our external family system. The External Family Systems model has identified various roles that are played in families. The Internal Family Systems model does the same thing; it also identifies roles, but these roles exist internally, inside of us. Schwartz says we have a True Self, a capital S Self. In the church we call our True Self the *imago Dei*, and say we're made in the image of God. Schwartz would say there are parts, or subpersonalities, that surround the True Self. These parts hold stories, memories, and pain.

"For the well-adjusted person, the True Self is large and expansive. Someone like that most likely grew up in a home where they were supported, held, celebrated, and loved. Or, if they didn't grow up in a home like that, they've done a lot of inner work. In biblical terms, we'd say they demonstrate the fruit of the Spirit found in Galatians 5: love, joy, peace, patience, kindness, goodness, faithfulness, gentleness, and self-control. Similarly, Schwartz has identified eight self-leadership characteristics that all start with the letter "C": courage, calmness, creativity, compassion, confidence, clarity, curiosity, connectedness. These are markers of the True Self. I believe the Apostle Paul in Galatians and Richard Schwartz, in the Internal Family Systems model, are speaking of the same things. When a well-adjusted person experiences traumas in life, as everyone does, they are able to process those traumas."

Just as the Apostle Paul and Richard Schwartz use different language to describe the same thing, in *Telling Secrets*, Frederick Buechner speaks of the True Self: "I believe that what Genesis suggests is that this original self, with the print of God's thumb still upon it, is the most essential part of who we are and is buried deep in all of us as a source of wisdom and strength and healing."

Buechner goes on to speak of our other selves—often so many selves that it's as if "we are constantly putting on and taking [them] off like coats and hats against the world's weather."

Chuck calls these multiple selves the divided self.

"For people who have experienced significant pain," Chuck said, "where the pain or abuse has not been processed by the True Self, where it is held within us in the absence of a compassionate witness, what ends up happening is that pain gets compartmentalized. We've got a slot here, another slot here, another here, and here, and here.

"Let's say you were sexually abused when you were 8 years old. There's a part of you that holds that pain. Imagine that pain has never been processed but suppressed. In that moment when you were abused when you were 8, your brain flooded with the stress hormone cortisol, which took your ability to explicitly remember the event offline and implicitly encoded it in your body. Let's say you get married and have sex for the first time on your honeymoon night and all those memories come flooding back, which introduces a lot of anguish into what should have been a wonderful time. You wind up lying on your bed sobbing, curled in a fetal position, not understanding what's happening. It's because of how your body was holding the abuse. That's the sort of scenario that happens with compartmentalized pain. We're just now beginning to understand the science of how the parts of our brains function and the effects of stress hormones like cortisol on how our brains are wired."

As we talked, Chuck returned repeatedly to recent discoveries in brain science. He laughed and said, "One hundred years from now we'll have all this figured out. We'll crack the genetic codes, unravel the mysteries of nature and nurture, and know exactly how and why the brain reacts and responds in different situations. We are discovering a lot."

We do live in an age of discovery. There is an amazing amount of literature being published on discoveries in brain science and how we process trauma. A book that has helped build my understanding of brain science and trauma is Bessel van der Kolk's *The Body Keeps the Score: Brain, Mind, and Body in the Healing of Trauma.* Van der Kolk writes: "Trauma is not just an event that took place sometime in the past; it is also the imprint left by that experience on mind, brain, and body. This imprint has ongoing consequences for how the human organism manages to survive in the present."

~

I began to see that it isn't that we don't process pain, but that we process it differently and hold it in different places.

Chuck went on to share an example of how extreme compartmentalization can become, citing a person he worked with who had dissociative identity disorder (previously referred to as multiple personality disorder). This person had been repeatedly sexually abused as a child by her father, who would recite the Lord's Prayer as he was abusing her. As an adult, the woman appeared at counseling sessions as someone named Andrea. After one of their sessions, Chuck received an email from one of Andrea's "alters," a separate self from Andrea. This alter wrote Chuck and said, "Andrea is in more danger than she knows, but I'm looking out for her."

At one point, the alter wrote Chuck and said, "Andrea was supposed to sign a contract today, but she couldn't handle it, so I went in and did it for her." She had another alter called "Raging Fury" who reported Andrea had been raped one night after visiting a gym. Andrea was not aware that she'd been raped or aware of many other events that happened to her. She only knew that she'd lost pockets of time. Her brain was organizing her experiences to keep her from being overwhelmed by those experiences. Dissociative identity disorder was the brain's survival strategy, stemming from the abuse she'd experienced as a child.

In a less extreme example of compartmentalization, Chuck mentioned a client who had given Disney character names to her parts. Ursula was her dominant part, arrogant and forceful, Rapunzel was a little girl locked in a tower, and Snow White was the naïve part of her who continually put herself into the presence of patriarchal and abusive men. In this example, the client was fully aware of her parts and was working on befriending and being compassionate toward them.

Narcissistic tendencies are another way we protect ourselves from pain. Narcissism typically is rooted in childhood abuse. A grandiose personality with very high castle walls gets built. The walls lock away the pain and may be fortified with a large and extraordinary defense system. Narcissism becomes the only game the person knows, preferring to go on the offensive, monopolizing and bullying and refusing to accept defeat or pain. In therapy it's often hard for this person to access other parts of themselves. The therapist will say, "Surely, there's more to you than this," and the narcissist will answer, "No, this is me."

Labels like "narcissist" can become problematic, though.

"I'm very cautious about pathologizing people," Chuck said. "People are always more than a label. Most all of us have narcissistic parts. But what the DSM (the *Diagnostic and Statistical Manual of Mental Disorders*, published by the American Psychological

Association, the authoritative tool for making psychiatric diagnoses) classifies as narcissistic personality disorder—which is characterized by an inflated sense of self-importance, a deep need for admiration, and a lack of empathy—is a matter of degree. The diagnosis can be helpful in some situations, but it's never the whole of someone. People with full-blown narcissistic personality disorder don't always appear that way. They are often unpredictable; we don't know which part will show up when. What's significant for the question about how we process pain is that narcissistic behavior is a way of dealing with pain. A little boy—and most people with narcissistic personality disorder are men—was hurt and this is how he's making sure he isn't hurt again. It may be maladaptive, but it's a way of trying to get our needs met.

$$\approx$$

Richard Schwartz published a book in 2021 entitled *No Bad Parts: Healing Trauma and Restoring Wholeness with the Internal Family Systems Model*. His emphasis on "no bad parts" moves away from the shame associated with labeling and pathologizing.

"I carry inside me," Chuck said, "an image of myself as an 8-year-old on the other side of a wall as my dad comes home between midnight and 2 a.m. I am listening as my mom yells at him, and they get into a fight. I'm in a fetal position, pounding on the wall, crying out, 'Don't get a divorce.' That little guy is still alive, and he can awaken in moments when I feel threatened. I might have an awkward conversation with my wife and that little boy who fears being abandoned will surface. I need to have a conversation with that little boy, to bring him online, and tell him he's welcome in the inner family, that he has a place at the table. Every part of me is welcome, including my inner Pharisee and my inner exile. The parts of me that are anxious and rude and judgmental and stubborn, the parts that are young and ashamed—all of them are me, and all of them have a place at the table. For me, the attraction of the Internal Family Systems model comes because it is based on compassion instead of shame. There's no judging of these parts, just acceptance and recognition of them."

In the Internal Family Systems model, there are protective parts and exile parts. The protective parts appear as both managers and firefighters, which use different coping strategies to protect us from pain. We have multiple manager parts, and they usually function well. They are the parts of us that are achievers, that keep the shop running and stay busy. They get along with life.

As Chuck spoke, he mentioned his ability to flip into manager mode. "I may be having a rough day where I'm dealing with social anxiety and shame-filled narratives are working inside of me. Let's say there's a faculty meeting that day. I am probably not going to show up to the faculty meeting that way. I'm going to show up in manager mode, showing the part of me that looks competent and like he belongs on a faculty. I will be my smart, academic self. Sometimes I might be really feeling like I don't belong—one way I deal with the insecurity of that is by cracking jokes and being funny. Sometimes Funny Chuck shows up at a meeting alongside Smart Chuck. Or maybe, if I don't fully get out of the exile mode, I'll probably just stay quiet in the meeting."

Exiles hold shame and pain. Exiles are sealed off and long to take cover and escape. They carry our burdens and our stories of abuse. Managers work to protect the exile. In therapy, the therapist starts working with the manager, because people won't show the exile right away. Therapists work through the manager to get to the exile. The other protective part Schwartz identifies is the firefighter. Firefighters go into overdrive when the exile is under threat and the manager doesn't seem to be able to handle it. Firefighters douse the pain of the exile with something that will work quickly to make the pain go away. Firefighters may drink the night away or medicate the pain by binging on food or pornography. Addictions can develop when this way of self-medicating forms neural pathways. We're also genetically prone to addictions, if our parents or grandparents struggled with addictions, we're more prone to use this way of dealing with pain.

At the worse, firefighters deal with pain by extinguishing a person's life altogether.

"I don't believe," Chuck said, "that a True Self takes its own life. I believe suicide comes from a part of us that says, 'I'll take care of this for you, I'll make the pain go away forever.'"

~

I asked Chuck how it is that different people who have experienced the same trauma can have such different reactions. What about, for example, three siblings who grow up in a family with parents who abused alcohol? As adults, the oldest seems on edge all the time, the middle child is disconnected from her siblings, and the third is easy going and serene.

"But did they really grow up in the same family?" Chuck asked. "Family roles are different. Maybe the older sibling was drawn into a role where he or she was protecting the younger siblings. He or she still over-functions. The middle sibling checks out, the younger sibling says, 'My childhood was fine,' while the oldest says, 'My childhood was hell.'

"Or consider this. I worked with a couple who had two very different responses to the same events, a husband and wife who had been through church trauma from a narcissistic leader. The husband came from a securely attached home. He had a family that celebrated the good times and gave comfort in the bad times. His wife, on the other hand, came from a family where her dad took his life when she was 2. She was sexually abused between the ages of

8 and 10. She's done a lot of inner work, but life still feels like she's swimming upstream much of the time. She's got more work to do. The husband is fit, put together, a muscular former football player, a 'glass half-full kind of guy'. She's a 'life is hard and bad things happen to us over and over' kind of person. The ministry couple that recruited them into the church hurt them. The husband says, 'Yeah, that was hard', and is able to walk me through all the events sequentially, from beginning to end, without any problem. He'd say, 'That made me sad', or 'That really hurt, but I can see the pastor's perspective'. His wife narrated what happened in fits and starts and pieces were simply too painful for her talk about. She'd repeatedly say, 'How come these things happen to us?'

"As I looked at her, I could see tension, so I asked her, 'What's happening in your body right now?' She described a surge that went up her neck and into her face, and said, 'My blood is boiling and my head's about to explode, and I just want to choke somebody.' Something was happening, she was experiencing a complex PTSD episode that compounded the trauma from over the course of her life. Meanwhile, her husband, with his secure attachment, can name and honor the various emotions he feels but is not drawn into the depths of pain. He's not flooded by it. Those are two people narrating the same thing very differently."

I asked if this could help explain why tragedy, like the loss of a child, may drive some couples apart instead of bringing them together.

"Certainly," Chuck said. "The different ways we narrate what happened can lead to tension. In the couple I worked with, he would say, 'It wasn't so bad', and she'd say, 'This is a cycle of abuse.' Meanwhile, he's trying hard to understand the pastor's point of view and understand a larger story. It's complicated and it's not as if one is telling it rightly and the other is telling it wrongly.

"We're learning a lot about trauma—in many ways we're on the front edges of understanding how trauma affects our bodies. The body keeps the score,' is more than just the name of a book, it's a true statement about trauma. It's one thing to tell a story, it's another to listen to your body. Richard Schwartz calls this a trailhead, a pathway for understanding what's happening inside of us. For example, I was in a meeting the other day and noticed some discomfort in my stomach. I got out my journal and personified my stomach and asked it what was going on. 'Okay tummy,' I wrote, 'what's happening with you?' 'Why are we here right now?' it asked me. So we got into a dialogue that was helpful. I figured out why I felt the way I did by following the trailhead that began with a body sensation."

～

Chuck's emphasis on how much of our ability to process pain is related to childhood experiences made me think of Nadine Burke Harris' book *The Deepest Well: Healing the Long-Term Effects of Childhood Adversity*. Harris is a medical doctor, not a psychologist, specializing in public health. She's also a great storyteller. At points, her book is like a detective novel as she works to unravel the mystery of what's really happening with the patients she sees.

Harris uses an inventory called the ACE test, which measures adverse childhood experiences. The ACE test scores ten factors:

- Recurrent emotional abuse
- Recurrent physical abuse
- Sexual abuse
- Physical neglect
- Emotional neglect
- Substance abuse in the household
- Mental illness in the household
- Mother treated violently

- Divorce or parental separation
- Criminal behavior in the household

The higher someone's ACE score, the more likely they are to have negative outcomes. What's revelatory in Harris' work is that she's not only tracking mental health outcomes but overall health outcomes. Research shows ACEs happen regardless of geography, ethnicity, or socioeconomic background. ACEs are no respecter of class or race, and most of the population has experienced at least one ACE. High ACE scores in children are predictors of behavioral problems and the diagnosis of ADHD. They also are predictors of obesity, asthma, diabetes, pneumonia, and other medical issues. Most physicians treat these illnesses case by case, symptom by symptom, without ever putting the fuller picture together. As adults, people with high ACE scores are much more likely to have strokes, heart disease, and cancer.

Harris uses the example of a child touching a hot stove to illustrate how the brain sorts data through the body's stress-response system. The brain biochemically marks the stove as dangerous, and when encountering a hot stove in the future the child will experience warning signs that include vivid memories, muscle tension, and rapid pulse that convince the child not to touch the hot stove again.

Harris writes that sometimes the stress response works overtime. What saved a life in one context can be damaging in another. This is seen in combat soldiers who return from the front lines with post-traumatic stress disorder (PTSD). For these veterans, and others with PTSD, the past has made it difficult to live in the present. The noise of a jet filled with tourists is mistaken for that of a bomber. "The problem with PTSD," Harris writes, "is that ... the stress response is caught in the past, stuck on repeat."

Our bodies remember and do keep the score. Our stress-response systems allow us to survive; a stress-response system that is not negatively affected by ACEs will help save us. But when the stress-response system has been negatively affected by ACEs, that same system can shorten lives. Stress can be positive—it helps us get up for big moments. We focus more intently as more oxygen is delivered to the heart and lungs, allowing peak performance. But over time, adverse experiences release stress hormones that can damage the brain's architecture, weaken the immune system, and damage other organs. Harris notes the body is like "one big, intricate Swiss watch," and what happens in one part affects other parts.

One study Harris cites, conducted by Dr. Victor Carrion, a child psychiatrist and the director of the Stanford Early Life Stress and Resiliency Program, used MRI technology to see the effects of the stress hormone cortisol on kids who had experienced trauma. The study was able to show measurable changes to brain structure and found that the more trauma a child had experienced, the higher the cortisol levels and the smaller the volume of the child's hip-pocampus, a part of the brain intimately involved in learning and memory. A year later, the shrinkage of the hippocampus continued, even though the child was no longer experiencing trauma.

As this study indicates, complications that stem from trauma may relate to actual changes to the brain and are not the result of the child's bad behavior or a lack of willpower.

One factor that helps children weather and survive adverse experiences is quality and caring relationships with adults. This is not only true for children, as van der Kolk explains in *The Body Keeps the Score*: "Study after study shows that having a good support network constitutes the single most powerful protection against becoming traumatized. ... Frightened adults respond to the same comforts as terrified children: gentle holding and rocking and the assurance that somebody bigger and stronger is taking care of things, so you can safely go to sleep."

On the flip side, consider the interactions with adults mentioned earlier. My friend's father found that his mother had committed suicide in the family garage and then was emotionally abused by his father. Andrea was sexually abused by her father as he recited the Lord's Prayer. The woman from the couple who faced abuse at church survived the suicide of her mother and was sexually abused. All of them experienced multiple ACEs without comfort and security from loving relationships. All of them struggled to process pain in a healthy way as adults. Since relationships are so important to healing trauma, relationship-based trauma is more complex and more difficult to treat.

When the very people who are supposed to take care of you abuse you, the brain takes its own steps to protect you. As *The Deepest Well* illustrates, this isn't just a mental health issue. Nadine Burke Harris, as a public health physician, is working to get ACE tests into physicians' offices and health clinics. Those with high ACE scores often present with health problems. Yet they need holistic treatment that isn't only focused on symptoms but looks at the complete picture. Treatment plans for those with multiple ACEs may include diverse elements such as talk therapy, medication, nutrition interventions, yoga, and other mindfulness techniques.

The good news is that even though humans have the ability to destroy each other, we also have the ability to heal each other. The same species that created the people who flew airplanes into the Twin Towers of the World Trade Center produced the firefighters who ran up the stairs of those towers, sacrificing all to save others. The worst and the best of human behaviors are inside of us. When I think of the divided self or our multiple selves I think positively of Walt Whitman saying, "I contain multitudes" and negatively of the demon saying to Jesus, "My name is Legion, for we are many."

~

As we've seen in earlier chapters, Roger Nelson, Quentin Henry, and Mitch Kinsinger demonstrate remarkable resilience. I asked Chuck DeGroat to help me understand resilience and where it comes from.

"Resilience comes as we live out of our True Self," Chuck said. "Resilient people are not as prone to be flooded by their emotions. I call this wholeheartedness. The Apostle Paul called it the 'new self.' It means living less out of the shadows. The True Self is more spacious, more free, more able to define what its emotions are without being dominated by those emotions. It can speak of sadness without becoming that sadness. The True Self can speak of feeling anger without becoming anger. My True Self can speak on behalf of my anger.

"I've had people I've worked with say to me, 'I used to be a category five hurricane. Then I got to a category three hurricane. Now I am living in the quiet eye of the storm. I'm not the storm anymore.' That's the birthplace of resilience, a place where we know ourselves, are known by others, and known by God. Others are important—an important part of resilience is having friends who will speak truth to you. In my early years on a faculty another faculty member would say, 'I noticed you didn't say anything in the faculty meeting today. What's up?' That was important.

"Maladaptive ways of coping fade as the True Self emerges. It's hard for some people to access the True Self—as I've said, narcissists especially have a hard time accessing the True Self. For people who have internalized pain as trauma, the parts are all very active, often very reactive, and can't get to a state of being fully present. The True Self can connect deeply to other people, but when you're living out of your parts, you're living self-protectively and compartmentalized.

"In therapy, we're not trying to get rid of our parts. We want to help people recognize and welcome their parts. So many Christians are ashamed, for example, that they experience lust and want to destroy that part of them. But there's no need to be ashamed and no need to destroy that part. It just wants love. Or let's say one way you cope is by being busy. If you're busy enough, you don't have time to feel your pain. Well, there's nothing wrong with being busy and working hard. That can be very valuable. We want to avoid the dualistic, binary thinking that labels your busy self as bad. We're not trying to extinguish it, instead we're asking, how can you befriend it? Can you enter a new relationship with your busy self—can it back away from a position of control and find a new role? Can you repurpose your busy self and not let it take over? This type of self-care and self-love is not narcissistic. It's having compassion on yourself. It's a way of healing. Can the true self drive the bus instead of your busy self?

"It's important to recognize that we're not expecting a one-time transformation. This is the work of a lifetime. We have these parts that make superhero efforts to save the exile within. They don't have to. A truly integrated person can channel their strengths and look at their vulnerabilities with tenderness."

I asked, "Then, where do the common problems of anxiety and depression fit in?"

Chuck started by saying that anxiety and depression are ultimately mysteries, part of the nature/nurture conundrum that has fueled so much argument and speculation. Anxiety and depression are most likely biological traits that get unleashed by life experiences. Why they emerge in some and not others, or to the degree they emerge, or when they emerge are all mysteries—part of the genetic and brain science we are starting to unlock.

"Anxiety is a way to deal with life's contingencies," Chuck said, "and it can keep us distant from our pain. For high achievers, anxiety can be the fuel that powers them, but it may sabotage others.

As a therapist, I don't deal with anxiety abstractly, on its own, but as it relates to our parts. Most likely anxiety is encoded within us during childhood. There are drugs that can provide relief and help people, but at the same time those drugs may mask the real issues.

"Regarding depression—it's important to distinguish depression from sadness. Not all sadness is depression. There can be resilient, True Self sadness that coincides with tragedy. That's not the same as depression, which can take the driver's seat and become a sort of black cloak that envelops someone and makes it impossible to get out of bed. That kind of depression isn't necessarily related to a specific event. The DSM specifies what depression is—the key question is, how pervasive is it? As with anxiety, there are medications to help people with depression. And as with the other things we've talked about, depression is another way—albeit a maladaptive way—to deal with pain."

As our conversation wound down, Chuck brought up Frederick Buechner's concept of burying pain.

"Buechner has a gift for using layman's language to describe profound concepts," Chuck said. "When we bury pain, we cut parts of our selves off from other parts. Here's an example of what I mean: Some of us are so compartmentalized we only live from the head up. This is an exaggeration, but it's like someone being so out of touch with their body that they wonder, what's this moisture coming from my eyes? As we engage and truthfully tell our stories, we become more integrated and pull away the layers so we may become a whole person, able to hold pain and joy together, able to hold complexity and embrace oneness.

"That's resilience, being able to hold more than one emotion at a time. And that's wholeheartedness—when we integrate head, heart, and body. That's the goal and the work of a lifetime."

Chuck DeGroat is Professor of Pastoral Care and Spiritual Formation at Western Theological Seminary. www.ChuckDeGroat.net

8

Suicide and Soulwork

"I had a propensity to believe the world was perfect, I was perfect, my family was perfect, and my marriage was perfect. Of course, it wasn't perfect—there was a real disconnect between the way I wanted the world to be and how it actually was."

Poet Rosemerry Wahtola Trommer

"People doing a regular soulwork practice may already have the tools and wherewithal to begin processing a cataclysmic event in both a faster and better way than others."

The Rev. Sophie Mathonnet-VanderWell

Each day, I look forward to an email containing a poem by Rosemerry Wahtola Trommer—a discipline Rosemerry maintains with remarkable perseverance and courage.

When I learned that she has the slightly eccentric habit of occasionally writing lines of poetry on rocks, I approached her at a workshop with a Sharpie pen and a rock in my hands and asked her to write something beautiful I could give to my wife.

Rosemerry wrote:

You and I

two threads joined

in one miraculous cloth

I took my rock home feeling like husband of the year.

Her poetry is accessible and insightful. She's won poetry prizes; she's had poems in *O Magazine* and on *The Prairie Home Companion*—and she's been poet laureate of Colorado's western slope. That day at the workshop, Rosemerry spoke about how sending out a poem a day changed her relationship to poetry from a product to a practice. The practice depends on Rosemerry not just showing up but finding language appropriate for each day. Her mantra is, "It doesn't have to be good, but it does have to be true."

I left the workshop not just inspired to write poetry, but thinking a lot about how my life would be different if I fully lived into a daily practice that kept me grounded, and where I would be if I focused on telling the truth instead of trying to impress others. I thoroughly enjoyed that day with Rosemerry and looked forward to reading her daily offerings.

Then, the poems stopped in mid-August 2021. After almost two weeks of silence, a message came on August 26: "This is the most difficult time of my life. My beautiful, beloved boy, Finn Thilo Trommer, killed himself on Saturday, August 14. He would have turned 17 on September 11." She went on to say that although Finn had extraordinary energy and talent, since the day he was born he carried a deep unease. "He shined so brightly, I believe, because he had to summon that much luminosity just to meet the darkness that was ever inside him. And so although the inner struggle is what eventually killed him, I refuse to vilify it, because it is also what shaped him into the radiant and magical being he was. ... He was a comet. Astonishingly brilliant and then gone. I pray every day now that he finds the peace he never had in this life.

I pray that peace finds him. That he feels what it is to know no lack. To know his own beauty and sufficiency."

I was deeply moved by the openness of what she sent. In our culture, suicide is stigmatized and shameful, and we struggle to find words to talk openly about it. This was different. Rosemerry calls herself the "Wordwoman" online, and here she was using words to say things many of us struggle to articulate. I was also impressed by the wisdom and love she displayed when she said she refused to vilify the inner struggle that killed her son.

How long, I wondered, would it be before she would start sending out poems again?

The answer came a few weeks later when the poems resumed early in October. One of the first began:

> I am not the woman I was
>
> a year ago.

A day later a poem said:

> To meet grief is to be
> deeply steeped in love.

Poem after poem followed, most of them addressing Rosemerry's grief in one way or another. They were often heartbreaking, but somehow never too much. I resonated with a poem published in the beginning of 2022 that spoke of calling Finn's cell phone to hear the familiar sound of his voice:

> I hang up at the beep,
> and then I'm gasping,
> choking, making sounds
> I don't recognize.

The standard advice is to wait a while, to put off most things for at least a year following a traumatic loss. Writers are told to let time pass to gain perspective before trying to write about their experience. Again, a year is the general rule. But here was some-one not willing to wait, not willing to suffer her grief in isolation, someone intent on inviting her readers into that grief, regardless of the mess. Here was someone who chose to meet a loved one's suicide with openness and a willingness to turn toward it instead of away.

How did she have the strength to do this? Where did the cour-age to hold her pain to the light come from?

When I reached out to Rosemerry and asked those questions, she answered: "Poetry."

She said, "There is no doubt in my mind that my daily practice for fifteen years of being willing to show up and meet moment after moment after moment has helped me meet this challenge. To see what's happening in the world outside of us and feel what's happening in the world inside of us and be curious about that intersection is what the practice of poetry is all about. From the first moments after Finn's suicide, I prayed, 'Let me stay open. Let me meet this. I just want to meet it all.' The invitation of the poem is to meet whatever is happening and tell the truth about it."

I had so many questions about Finn, about why he chose to end his life, and about the impact of his decision on those around him. I reached out to Rosemerry not quite five months after Finn's sui-cide. I wondered if she'd be willing to talk to me—it was so fresh a wound—but I thought maybe, because of the poems she'd been sending out, she might be willing to answer my questions.

She did not hesitate. I'm tempted to say it was remarkable, but all of the conversations I've had with people whose stories I've told in this book have been remarkable. Yet none have come so soon after the traumatic event as the conversation I had with Rosemerry.

She described Finn as full of paradox. As a baby, he cried hard the first year of his life—not the first few weeks, or months, but a full year, and not for a bit of each day but for long periods. Doctors were unable to pinpoint the cause of his discomfort.

"It doesn't escape me," Rosemerry said, "that no matter how hard I tried to comfort him, the first year of Finn's life began with suffering."

He was always exceptional—a whirlwind of energy and force described as a toddler by a friend of Rosemerry's as "150% alive." He started preschool as a 4-year-old, and although Rosemerry feared Finn's energy would make him aggressive with other kids, he was sweet and gentle. His teachers described him as lovely and respectful and kind. He developed an outward persona that was helpful, radiant, and loving, but he could be much moodier and darker at home, where he felt safe to bring his whole self. His family knew well both his radiance and his darkness. Maybe whatever it was that made him cry that first year was still in there somehow.

He consistently received top grades in school and would pick up new activities and soon excel at them. He joined the school chess club and then won the chess tournament. He took up skiing and soon was skiing like a daredevil off cliffs. He began dancing in second grade—tap and hip hop and had started ballet before he died. He was graceful, long and lean at 6'4" (and still growing) and carried his lithe body with ease. He had a high degree of emotional intelligence and listened well to others. He could be playful and goofy and would moonwalk across the house at times, but at other times was full of struggle.

When he was in sixth grade, he began to talk about wanting to kill himself. His parents took him to a mental health crisis center. He began working with a therapist, whom Finn would continue to talk to until his suicide. Finn's initial diagnosis said that his problems stemmed from a combination of hormonal changes, depression, and perfectionism. As he grew, his parents tried lots of options to help him in addition to therapy. He met with a life coach, tried acupuncture, and the practice of qigong. When things became difficult at school, they enrolled him in a different school. His mother and he even took up fencing, to give his remarkable energy another outlet. He was also religiously inquisitive, first exploring Judaism and then Christianity. He had gone on a mission trip to a small town in Guatemala, and during the pandemic created a website to help the people of the town.

The perfectionism in his initial diagnosis seemed like a puzzle, but he became more and more rule-governed as he grew. He ate each food in a meal in a particular order, needed to have the pencils on his desk lined up just so, and became attracted to the discipline and rigor of the military, which he planned to join. He excelled at math and science and technology. His rule-following and perfectionist standards created tension with his friends. Living in Colorado, home of some of the most liberal marijuana laws in the country, he became staunchly against its use. He became angry with classmates who experimented with drugs or used alcohol, and expressed disappointment when friends didn't do their homework or follow through on something they had said they would do.

"Finn would get on them," Rosemerry said, "but they already had parents to do that. Not only was Finn disappointed by them, but he would let them know he was disappointed by them, and nobody likes that."

Friends told Finn they were tired of feeling like he was looking down on them. He had helped create an online group with his friends, where they hung out and played games together. Three weeks before his death, the others voted him out of the group and blocked his access, not realizing how sensitive he was. This was the boy who had cried and cried the first time his mother told him the story of Cinderella. He was incredibly sensitive, and filled with incredible energy, which he often didn't know what to do with. The problems with his friends weighed heavily on him.

"Those kids made choices that were painful for Finn," Rosemerry said, "but we do not blame them for how Finn responded. They are not responsible for Finn's death."

∼

In August 2021, Rosemerry, her husband, Eric, Finn, and his 13-year-old sister, Vivian, traveled to Georgia to help Rosemerry's parents move into a senior living facility. Because of his troubles with his friends, Finn had applied to different boarding schools earlier in the year. By late summer he'd decided to stay at home in Colorado, but since one of the schools he had applied to was in Rome, Georgia, where Rosemerry's parents were moving, and since things with his friends had deteriorated so much, he decided to visit the school in Georgia. It was a Friday, and even though it was move-in day for the new year, the staff welcomed Finn and made it clear they were eager for him to be one of their students. Finn talked excitedly about going to school there and wanted his sister to go to school there also. He could see a path forward and a future for himself. He downloaded a picture of Auburn University, where he hoped to go to college, on his phone. He knew he had choices, which makes the events of the next day harder to fully comprehend.

On that day, August 14, Rosemerry and Eric went to the hardware store and Rosemerry's dad, whose kidneys were failing, went to dialysis. Rosemerry's mother invited Finn along when she went to pick her husband up, and after initially agreeing to go, Finn changed his mind and stayed in the new apartment his grandparents were moving into. Alone with Vivian, who was listening to music on her headphones, Finn went into the guest bedroom, which features a large walk-in closet. There were several boxes that needed to be dealt with in that closet, and there were guns in one of the boxes. Although the Trommers have no guns in their Colorado home, Rosemerry's father was a hunter and gun enthusiast. Finn took his phone and posted a message on Snapchat that said he was sorry for what he was about to do but that he had lost everything he ever had. He told his family that he loved them and then said that his friends had turned on him, but it was his own fault. He said he had tried to change but couldn't.

After finishing the message, he took one of his grandfather's guns, sat down in the threshold between the room and walk-in closet, and removed the rings he was wearing and meticulously arranged them in a line on the floor. And then 16-year-old Finn Thilo Trommer chose to take his own life.

Vivian heard the gunshot muffled by her headphones and thought something had fallen. She went to check and found Finn. She had the presence of mind to press the emergency call button in the bathroom, call 911, text her grandparents telling them not to come home, and then call her mother and tell her Finn had shot himself. Later, Vivian recovered Finn's phone and took down the Snapchat message. Remarkably, she texted a message to Finn from her own phone, telling him she loved him and asking him to stay because things would get better. Then she used Finn's phone to send herself a message, saying that he loved her and was proud of her, and was sorry that she had to see him like this.

As a parent, I have marveled that my children, made from the same genetic material, have such different personalities. That certainly was the case with the Trommer children. Whereas Finn was never content or satisfied, Vivian has an even temperament that gave her the ability, amid emotional anguish and through her tears, to sequentially do what needed to be done.

"I am in awe of how she handled the first day," Rosemerry said, "and aware that she carries a different burden than the rest of us."

"There are ways," Rosemerry said, "that Finn prepared me for this. Before I became pregnant with him, I had a propensity to believe the world was perfect, I was perfect, my family was perfect, and my marriage was perfect. Of course, it wasn't perfect—there was a real disconnect between the way I wanted the world to be and how it actually was. There was also a disconnect between what I projected to the world and how I was. It was delusional. Finn forced me to change—when he was born and screamed for a year, there was no pretending anything was perfect. He was in pain, and I could not do a thing about it. He was born a month early, and I couldn't do anything about that either. Finn forced me to meet the world as it is, instead of as how I wished it to be. He did that every day of his life. He was such a button pusher. I could never delude myself into thinking everything was perfect ever again. Even in taking his own life—which is the last thing in the world I would have wanted—Finn is inviting me again to meet the world as it really is. He's been teaching me to do that his whole life.

"Another remarkable thing, which cannot be overstated, is how much love I have felt at this time. This might sound weird, but from the day Finn died I have felt what I call an 'onslaught of love.' Much of that has come from the loving responses of so many people, but more than that I have felt love come over me—a huge rush of love. I had a moment of saying, 'No, no, no, this is too much, I can't take it,' but love obliterated that. It has infused me and held me—for the first two months I had a feeling of being held, a constant squeezing around my chest, like life itself, or love, was saying, 'I've got you.' Love has met me every step of the way. I never knew this could happen. All of this love—this unfathomable grace—has allowed me to meet each moment and has supported me all the time. I trust it completely."

Two weeks after Finn died, Rosemerry was back in Colorado and decided to go for a walk on a local trail. She had cocooned in her house immediately after Finn's death but going outside for walks helped. On this day, there was a car parked near the trail-head and the father of one of the boys who had shunned Finn was sitting inside the parked car.

"I don't blame those boys for what happened," Rosemerry said. "Finn is the one who took his own life, and he knew he had other choices." Still, she wasn't sure she was ready to see one of those other parents. Not sure what to do, she started walking past the car but then stopped and tapped on the window.

The man got out and said, "I am so sorry. I cry every day thinking about what happened."

Rosemerry hugged him and said, "I love you and I love your son."

"There is no way," Rosemerry said, "that I was strong enough to knock on that window on my own and there is no way I had enough love in me to be loving with him. That was the first of many moments when I realized that I don't have to do anything. Meeting that moment took zero effort on my part. Love rises up and helps me meet anything. Love does the work and says the right things. I am not alone. I am divinely met. I don't have to do it. Love does it. This is life changing in every way."

It's easy for me, as someone who identifies as a Christian, to hear all of this as a Christian story. I am quick to fill in the blanks and am positive I know the source of the overmastering love that Rosemerry has experienced.

While Rosemerry is open to those possibilities, she isn't sure. Though raised Episcopalian, she says that while she's aware these epiphanies of love and grace are divine, she doesn't have a structure for them and isn't sure who God is.

I'm not the only one who wants to fill in the blanks for Rosemerry—her mother often says to her, "Sweetheart, you are full of the Holy Spirit." I agree with Rosemerry's mother.

Rosemerry has met monthly with the spiritual teacher Joi Sharp since 2009. Joi had emphasized saying yes to the world as it is, something Rosemerry understood conceptually but not in practice until Finn's suicide.

~

As 2021 progressed, Rosemerry's father's health continued to deteriorate, and Rosemerry returned to Georgia in mid-November. Although eager to see her father, Rosemerry was not sure she was ready to walk into the space where Finn had taken his own life. Her mind filled with the image of returning from the hardware store and seeing the ambulance outside.

"I got out of the car," Rosemerry said, "and sat down on the grass and just cried and cried."

Rosemerry told her mother she felt like she needed to get a hotel room for the night. But there was a film festival happening in town, and the nearest vacant hotel room was about forty-five minutes away.

"It seemed so perfect," Rosemerry said, "that life was again showing me that I'm not in charge. It was a reminder to be open. 'Of course,' I thought, not in a sarcastic way, but in a 'Life-I-am-on-board-with-you' kind of way. I felt very unsettled going back into my parents' home. I told my mom I needed a lot of space. When we walked in the door, I immediately ran to that threshold where Finn had been. When I sat down there, I felt an instantaneous calm—but it wasn't a peaceful calm. It was sterile, whitewashed, all zeroes and ones. I felt as if I was having the kind of experience Finn had when he sat there. I didn't move for a long time, feeling that very rational, cold, clear, resolute space. I was being given the gift of feeling what it was like for him in those last moments. I did what he did. I took off all my rings and laid them on the floor in a neat row in front of me. I put my finger to my head and imagined making that choice. I said to Finn that I honored his choice. I hated it but I honored it. I understood that he believed things would not get better. Throughout his life, he felt like he was in a burning building, and he had no reason to believe it was going to do anything but get hotter. He was so methodical, rational, and precise. This was a very conscious choice that he made, and I believe he wasn't just saying no to this world but saying yes to another one."

When I asked Rosemerry if she had "what if" or "if only" kind of thoughts, she said that life had put up some guardrails for her—like those bumpers bowling alleys use to prevent gutter balls.

"Any time I go into the past," she said, "with 'what if,' or likewise if I go into the future with 'I'll never' kind of thoughts, like 'I'll never see him graduate' or 'I'll never know what his children would have looked like,' it is extremely painful. But to stay in the present, with the pain in the present, there is a lot of beauty in that. The beauty of grief has been a discovery. It's like the sound of a cello playing in a minor key: aching, painful, and so beautiful. Grief is being totally present with your love for someone no longer with you. The loss of that physical presence is painful but charged with so much love it's beautiful. Either side of it—going into the past or projecting into the future—is like fingernails on a chalkboard. Life is saying, 'Don't go there,' and keeping me on track."

Another aspect of how Rosemerry has met Finn's suicide came to her early on when the story Rosemerry was telling herself changed.

"Initially," she said, "I was stuck on 'Now I am the mother of a boy who killed himself.' I didn't like the way that felt. It was self-pitying and full of shame. I hated that story, but it kept playing in my head, over and over again."

A different story came to her. "In the morning," she said, "after a couple of sleepless nights, a voice said, 'I am the mother who learns how to love him now.' That was such a different story. It was a story that filled me with love and potential and goodness. That reframe, thankfully, happened quickly. It was a very important part of laying the groundwork that helped me meet this instead of shutting down. The story I tell myself is so important for staying open to it."

Rosemerry echoes a point Mary Anderson made—the story we tell ourselves, the story we believe we are in, makes a difference.

~

I processed the story of Finn and Rosemerry with the Rev. Sophie Mathonnet-VanderWell. After being born and raised in Japan by French parents, Sophie has spent her adult life in the United States and has been a pastor for almost four decades, serving churches in New York and Iowa. I wanted to particularly process the spiritual aspects of Rosemerry's story with a pastor and chose Sophie because I knew that as a long-tenured pastor, she'd dealt with suicide in her congregations.

When Sophie was a young pastor in New York, a woman named Laura was in her church. Laura's husband, Fred, belonged to a different church, about forty miles away from Sophie's church. Although Sophie did not know Fred well, one day she was asked to make a pastoral call on Laura and Fred. She learned Fred had had a recurrence of cancer that most likely would take his life. He and Laura had called Sophie to ask if Sophie's church might host Fred's funeral, since most of their friends were in that area. Sophie took the request to her board of elders, who approved it, and Sophie was able to share that information with Fred and Laura midweek. That Saturday, while Laura was out grocery shopping, Fred sat down at their kitchen table and shot and killed himself.

It became clear that Fred had been planning to kill himself, and securing the location for his funeral was a final step in his plan. Sophie was on the scene a few minutes after Laura discovered Fred's body. She stayed with Laura for several hours, and then

If you or a loved one are struggling with thoughts of suicide, call the national suicide-prevention hotline at 988. Visit 988lifeline.org for more information.

hosted a bishop and priest from Fred's church for a few days while they prepared for a difficult funeral.

That would not be the last time Sophie was intimately involved with a family after a suicide. A little over a decade ago, Sophie and her husband, Steve, who serves as co-pastor with Sophie in their church in Iowa, received a call from the local police saying there had been a death in the home of a family from their congregation. The police asked if one of the pastors would go to the home and the other accompany the police to tell the deceased's mother, who was not at home. Steve went to the home and learned that a short time earlier, a 22-year-old member of their church named Tommy had shot and killed himself in the basement laundry room.

Sophie went with the police to tell Tommy's mother and bring her home. For the next few days, Sophie accompanied the family through the process of waiting for the police to release the body, making arrangements at the funeral home, and holding the funeral. Tommy had been arrested for drunk and disorderly conduct the night before he shot himself. It wasn't his first arrest; he'd had a few run-ins with the police for this sort of behavior. His father had bailed him out of jail that morning and had told Tommy things were going to be all right, that they would work through this together. When he went upstairs, Tommy found a rifle and shot himself. His suicide came as a surprise and shock.

There are approximately one million suicides worldwide each year, and while each person and each story are unique, there often are common elements. The person who kills himself or herself chooses suicide as the best option to end the pain they are experiencing. Earlier, Chuck DeGroat said that a True Self doesn't take its own life, but the impulse comes from a part of us that says, "I can take care of this and make the pain go away forever."

Suicide may end that pain, but it spreads pain then onto those who loved that person. Family and friends are left to bear the weight of it. The routine of daily life is instantly turned into mourning and grief. Shock, numbness, and a long list of questions are all common in the wake of a suicide. It's been said that suicide puts both a question mark and an exclamation point where a period should be at the end of the sentence that was a life. Those left behind must come to grips with not knowing more, have to forgive themselves for not saying the perfect thing to prevent the suicide (even though there is no perfect thing to say), or perhaps forgive themselves for saying the wrong thing, even though it felt like the right thing to say at the time. Eventually, those left behind need to forgive the person for doing what he or she did, forgive them for the sad and violent way they ended their life, and forgive God for not stopping it. For Tommy's father; Fred's wife, Laura; and Finn's sister, Vivian; there is also the special burden of being the first to see the maimed and broken body of someone they loved.

∾

"The way Rosemerry described what Finn did is precise," Sophie said, "like he'd thought it out. Fred had also planned what he was going to do—he had gotten the place for the funeral lined up and then waited for Laura to leave the house on a shopping trip. Tommy was more impulsive, but he felt a sense of failure after being in trouble with the law again. There is a sense in each case that they've come to the end of the rope. One was facing a long hard slog with a potentially terminal illness, another didn't see a way out from forever being pigeonholed as a law breaker, and Finn had been outcast by friends, and apparently didn't see an end to a difficult life ahead of him. We can never understand what goes on in people's minds, but for each there seemed to be no other way out, or maybe, this seemed like the best way out. It's clearly a choice being made."

As Sophie and I talked about Rosemerry's reaction to Finn's suicide, Sophie spoke about how Rosemerry's daily practice of poetry had prepared her to meet this event in ways others might not have been able to.

"I call it 'soulwork,'" Sophie said, "and Rosemerry has practiced for a very long time. The practice doesn't have to be poetry—in her case it is—but people doing a regular soulwork practice may already have the tools and wherewithal to begin processing a cataclysmic event in both a faster and better way than others. The ways in which Rosemerry could continue to love Finn while detesting what has happened, and to offer love instead of blame to the young people (and their parents) who had shut Finn of out their group, show Rosemerry has done a lot of soulwork."

Again, to use the language Chuck DeGroat used, soulwork is a route to the True Self, where resilience can be found. Soulwork is a key to becoming a good steward of your pain. Another example Sophie pointed to of how Rosemerry's soulwork had helped her came from how quickly Rosemerry was able to move from shame to love.

"Suicide is stigmatized," Sophie said, "although this varies by culture. In the Japanese culture I grew up in, suicide traditionally is not viewed with shame. Often it is viewed with honor. It's a different story in Western culture."

Some of the roots of Western culture's stigmatization of suicide are religious. Throughout the history of the church, suicide was not only classified as a sin—it was often called an unforgiveable sin, and people who had killed themselves were denied funerals and burial in the church. In the past few decades, though, various denominations have taken a more pastoral approach. For example,

Pope John Paul II approved the Catechism of the Catholic Church in the 1990s, which cited the role mental health plays in many suicides and includes language about not despairing over the eternal salvation of those who have taken their own life. Still, questions linger.

"When I was upstairs with Tommy's mother," Sophie said, "while the police were still in the basement with the body, Tommy's eternal destiny suddenly came to the surface. His mother asked if Tommy had committed an unforgivable sin. I told her that God's mercy was everlasting, and that seemed to comfort her.

"For pastoral reasons," Sophie said, "most people recognize it's been necessary for the church to move away from labeling suicide as a sin. We understand the mental health issues involved and that we can never fully get into the mind of someone who takes their own life. I'm happy the church has moved on this. Why it can't move on other issues puzzles me.

"It's been helpful for me, both personally and pastorally, to know that people are mysteries to be encountered, not problems to be fixed. If we can get to a place where we realize that sometimes our encounters with others have great beauty and other times great pain, we can let them be. That's what Rosemerry comes to. Finn is a mystery she continues to encounter, not a problem of guilt or shame to be fixed."

I'm reminded of a conversation I had with a friend who was in his 90s, who told me he'd had a disagreement the night before with his wife. She walked out of their apartment, and he asked, "Where are you going?"

She simply said, "Out."

He said to me, "I don't know where she went or what she did. I thought, 'Who is she?' We've been married seventy years and she is still a mystery to me. I don't completely know her."

No matter how much time we spend with another person, we'll never know their deepest thoughts and inner yearnings. Try as we might—and we do try passionately and profoundly to make ourselves known to each other—we find again and again that this is precisely what we cannot do. Mystery is at the center of every human heart. Most of our unanswered questions are because of these mysteries.

~

I asked Sophie about Rosemerry's ability to show compassion and forgiveness to the father of one of the boys who had shunned Finn. I doubt whether I could have done that so quickly—I imagine I might simply respond with anger.

"It is awe inspiring," Sophie said, "that Rosemerry was able to do that so soon after Finn's death. She admits she struggled at first—anyone would struggle—but then she knocked on that car window and was incredibly gracious. I bet that man was quaking in his boots, wondering what she was going to unload on him. I'm sure his first impulse was to flee, or if unable to do that, pretend she wasn't there. No one would relish that sort of encounter.

"Rosemerry acknowledged that for her to do what she did was not a product of her own strength but something else. She speaks of phenomena that Christians talk about without using the language Christians use. It would be patronizing of me to say she's a Christian when she does not identify herself that way, but she understands a certain way of being in the world, and a way of meeting the world, that Christians talk about. Christians say similar things like, "It wasn't me, it was the Spirit working inside me," or we speak of a forgiveness that is greater than ours, or of doing things not by our own strength."

One reason I'd particularly wanted to talk with Sophie was to get her reaction to Rosemerry's many spiritual expressions.

"She never says, 'Jesus got me through this,'" Sophie said, "but she is a very spiritual person. By that I mean that she is very in touch with her own spirit. More than that, she's not just incredibly spiritual, she's incredibly loving and she's incredibly forgiving. Those are categories Christians want to hold up. I've heard so many platitudes like, 'I don't know how people get through something like this without faith,' but the reality is I've sometimes seen Christians deal very poorly with difficult events and I've seen people who do not have faith—at least the faith we traditionally talk about—rise and meet life in gracious and healthy ways. We really should try to avoid platitudes. It's helpful for Christians to recognize God works beyond our categories. There are more mysteries in life than we can explain with our fairly simple, easily ordered theologies. That's something we can be grateful for. The stance that says, 'Unless they say it my way, it is not valid,' is insufficient. God is bigger than that. That doesn't mean I should not continue to say, "If it weren't for Jesus … "; but I can leave room for God to work beyond my categories. All of this is mystery—we know in part, but we don't know fully. We should hold these things lightly."

I was also curious if Sophie thought Rosemerry was writing about Finn and grief too soon, if she might have waited longer to get perspective, as conventional wisdom suggests.

"Rosemerry writes as a daily practice," Sophie said. "Unlike others, who might write to process their feelings after something traumatic, writing is a regular discipline in Rosemerry's life, and she's bringing this discipline to this event and its aftermath the same way she would bring this discipline to anything else. That's what's different here, and what allows her to not only write so soon after the event, but write with the sort of wisdom and compassion she has. She is willing to encounter and explore the mystery that was her son, dark shadows included."

It wasn't lost on me that Finn, an adolescent, living in that threshold space between childhood and adulthood, killed himself in a threshold between two different spaces. There is a symbolism there that Finn may not even have been consciously aware of. It reminds me of a scene in J. D. Salinger's classic novel *The Catcher in the Rye* where Holden Caulfield begins to have panic attacks trying to cross the streets in New York City. "I had this feeling I'd never get to the other side of the street. I thought I'd just go down, down, down, and nobody'd ever see me again."

Holden begins to imagine crossing the street with his younger brother Allie, who had died of leukemia three years before the beginning of the novel. He would ask Allie not to let him disappear as he crossed each street. This pattern repeated itself for many blocks as Holden moved uptown. It's easy to dismiss this as just a sign of Holden's instability, but I think Salinger was doing more. Childhood is one side of the street. Adulthood is the other. Adolescence is the street, the space between childhood and adulthood. Salinger was illustrating the difficulty Holden was having crossing the street from childhood to adulthood. Holden is not alone—many young people have difficulty crossing that street. Some never make it.

For Finn's family, an ordinary space where a walk-in closet adjoined a bedroom, a space that once had no particular meaning attached to it, is now charged with meaning and memory. Rosemerry rose to meet the challenge of returning to the scene of Finn's suicide, and I wondered what Sophie made of that visit and Rosemerry's reenactment of the event.

"I was surprised," Sophie said, "not so much by what she did but by what she felt or didn't feel. I expected this to be a hugely emotional space for her, instead she experienced a sort of death of feeling, similar to how Finn might have felt in the moment. That surprised me. But how can I know what it would feel like to be in her shoes? I think of Rosemerry going back to that place and then I think of Tommy's parents and the laundry room, or Laura and her kitchen. You are not going to stop using your kitchen or laundry room. I don't know how they have the strength to enter those spaces.

"Another aspect of Finn's story that breaks my heart is that a young person whose brain isn't fully developed, a young person whose impulse control isn't fully developed, is able to kill himself because a gun was right at hand. It was the same with Taylor. Fred was older, and a gun rights advocate, and I wonder if gun rights advocates realize that the guns they want for personal protection are so often used for suicide. Had a gun not been there, it doesn't mean the suicide would not have been attempted, but the means would have been less lethal, less deadly."

Finally, I asked Sophie how she saw God in Finn's story. "I see God everywhere in this story," she said. "It sounded like Finn may have had some obsessive-compulsive rigidity issues, which drew him to religion in ways the rest of his family were not drawn. Sadly, God was not a counterbalance to his legalistic tendencies. I wish it were different, but God is not a panacea for those who have mental health struggles.

"I also see God in the way Rosemerry has dealt with this event. She speaks of the divine, she even prays, but then she's not sure what to call these things—her mother calls it the Holy Spirit—and Rosemerry calls it love or grace. Those are good words. It is love and she has experienced grace. There's some kind of love and grace beneath everything. I go back to I Corinthians 13: Now we see in a mirror dimly, then we will see face to face. I wonder how it is that someone who does not define herself as a Christian can be so much more gracious and mature and forgiving than some Christians are. This is another mystery we all have to live with."

~

A few years ago, I was asked to officiate the funeral for a young man who had killed himself. The family did not have a minister and I was asked to fill that role. Of course, I said yes. But after saying that, I immediately wondered what I might say at the funeral. I didn't know the young man who had killed himself, or his family. They probably all just wanted to sit in a dark place and cry, but there we were, graveside on a hot summer day with clear blue skies and bright sunshine.

The family was full of shock and grief, and it was an incredibly sad scene. They were experiencing a sudden open wound that would never completely close. Because I did not know them and had not earned to right to speak to them, I leaned on the promises of scripture. Maybe I'm deceiving myself, but I believe there are miles of difference between empty religious platitudes and the promises of scripture. I told them that when the Apostle Paul said that nothing can separate us from the love of God in Jesus Christ, he was telling the truth. I told them that although they were bereft, they were not without hope, because Jesus Christ said he was the resurrection and the life. I told them that I believed the sufferings of this present time were nothing compared to the glory that awaits us, that there will come a day when God would wipe every tear from their eyes and that death would be no more, and mourning and crying and pain would be no more, and the one seated on the throne would say, "See, I make all things new."

And I told them what Isaiah said—that God would comfort all who mourn, and provide for all who mourn. I told them God promises a crown of beauty instead of ashes, and the oil of gladness instead of mourning.

I told them I believed their son and brother will wear a crown of beauty.

I believe the same is true for Finn Thilo Trommer.

Rosemerry Wahtola Trommer is a poet based in Southwestern Colorado. www.WordWoman.com

Sophie Mathonnet-VanderWell recently retired after more than three decades of pastoral ministry. She holds degrees from Seattle Pacific University and Princeton Theological Seminary and now lives in Des Moines, Iowa.

9

Living with Lament

"The voice of God calling upon the people to weep, lament, and mourn, for the calamities are about to descend upon them, is itself a voice of grief, a voice of weeping."
Abraham Joshua Heschel, The Prophets

"I resolved not to disown my grief, but to seek to own it redemptively— own it in such a way that might bring about some good."
Philosopher Nicholas Wolterstorff

"Some trauma is not possible to mend right away—it takes generations."
Makoto Fujimura

Nicholas Wolterstorff has a formidable presence. Undimmed in his 90s, with a full head of white hair, he possesses the serious, distinguished manner befitting the Noah Porter Professor Emeritus of Philosophical Theology at Yale University. He holds two advanced degrees from Harvard University, and, in addition to Yale, was a faculty member at both Calvin College (now University) and the Free University of Amsterdam. Nick has delivered named lecture series at universities around the world, including Oxford, St. Andrews, Princeton, and Yale. He had a formative role in creating the Society of Christian Philosophers and is the author of more than two dozen books on subjects as diverse as epistemology, ontology, art and aesthetics, justice, political philosophy, and metaphysics.

For all that, he may be best known for his slim volume *Lament for a Son*, published in 1987, following the tragic death of his son Eric in a climbing accident in Austria.

Eric was 25 years old at the time of the accident. He'd been a bright child who excelled at school. Adventuresome and curious, as a rising senior in high school he traveled on his own to take a summer course in ceramics at Alfred University in upstate New York. Between his sophomore and junior years of college, Eric traveled to Japan with friends and they freestyled their way through the country. In addition to his skill with ceramics, Eric was a talented musician, and had studied computer programming. He was excelling as a graduate student at Yale, supervising the discussion sections for the seven hundred undergraduate students in the introductory art history course, and at age 24 curated a show at Yale's British Art Museum. His dissertation focused on the origins of modern architecture, and in order to best study the work of the German architect Paul Schultze-Naumberg, Eric had rented rooms in Munich, which also put him close to his beloved Alps. Eric Wolterstorff loved mountain climbing.

He died doing what he loved.

Climbing solo fit Eric's venturesome personality—he took risks, did things independently, and was always moving ahead. "I would criticize him for driving too close to the car in front of him," his father said. "That's the way he was."

Eric died on June 11, 1983. When Eric's German landlady called and said that Eric was dead, his father had an image of holding Eric's limp body in his arms. Then he felt both intense cold and burning pain.

Nick traveled to Europe to claim Eric's body and retrieve Eric's possessions. On the way home, he had eight hours in the Luxembourg airport. "I had brought some things to read," Nick said, "but I couldn't read. So I took out some paper and started to write. I am a writer. That's what I do." Although he doubts a single sentence he wrote in the Luxembourg airport made it into *Lament for a Son*, the book's genesis happened that day.

Instead of writing about grief, Nick expressed his grief. The book, he would say, is a cry of grief. Among his lines:

> *"Sometimes I think that happiness is over for me."*
>
> *"My life is divided into before and after."*
>
> *"What do I do now with my regrets?"*
>
> *"The pain of the no more outweighs the gratitude of the once was. Will it always be so? I didn't know how much I loved him until he was gone. Is love like that?"*

Giving voice to grief through lament is mostly an ignored practice in the church. It hasn't always been that way—many of the Psalms are psalms of lament. They ask:

> *"How long?"*
>
> *"Why do you hide your face?"*
>
> *"Why have you forgotten me?"*

The lament of Psalm 102 (3-5) uses desperate poetic language:

> *For my days pass away like smoke,*
> *and my bones burn like a furnace.*
> *My heart is stricken and withered like grass;*
> *I am too wasted to eat my bread.*
> *Because of my loud groaning*
> *my bones cling to my skin.*

Lament raises its voice to say something is terribly wrong, something is not the way it's supposed to be. Modern American churches, either caught up in celebration and praise, or repeating the cycles of guilt and forgiveness, rarely practice lament. *Lament*

for a Son reintroduced this ancient practice for those touched by
Nick's wisdom. Eric's death wounded Nick, and the book expresses
the pain of that wound.

"We had plans with Eric," Nick said. "His brother Klaas was
going to spend the summer in Munich with him. We loved hearing
from Eric, talking with Eric. Now all of that was gone, leaving a
gaping void in its place."

"There's a hole in the world now," Nick wrote. "In the place where
he was, there's now just nothing ... The world is emptier. My son is
gone. Only a hole remains, a void, a gap, never to be filled."

In a sort of mockery, Eric's backpack and climbing boots were
unharmed. The authorities in Austria, however, suggested not
looking at the body. Later, at home, Nick's wife, Claire, insisted
they see and touch Eric's body.

"She was right," Nick said. "We saw him from the torso up.
Perhaps his lower body was mangled. It was important to touch
him, to see him." Not only are dead bodies disappearing from
funerals in our death-denying culture, funerals are disappearing
and being replaced by "celebrations of life." We want to glide past
death and not reckon with the bodies of the dead, yet there is
something elemental and primal about touching and seeing the
dead.

As Nick wrote: "I pity those who never get a chance to see and
feel the deadness of the one they love, who must think death but
cannot sense it. To fully persuade us of death's reality, and of its
grim finality, our eyes and hands must rub against death's cold,
hard body, body against body, painfully. Knowing death with mind
alone is less than fully knowing it."

True to his academic nature, Nick soon collected a pile of books
on grief so he could understand what was happening. He found
that he could not read them.

"I was not interested in Death," he said. "I was interested in Eric's
death."

Lewis Smedes, the author of several popular books of practical theology, gave the Wolterstorffs invaluable advice. "Lew Smedes said that you've heard there is company in misery," Nick said. "He told us that wasn't true, that instead grief isolates. This gave us the understanding and freedom to experience grief individually, at our own pace. Claire might be deep in grief on a day I felt like working in the garden. Or vice versa. Each of our children grieved differently. We had a common source of grief, but my grief was not their grief."

~

Lament for a Son has no chapters. There is no linear or narrative continuous flow to it. Its ragged nature reflects the ragged nature of grief. There is plenty of white space—Nick uses white space the way a poet uses white space—room is created for readers to supply their own thoughts. Over the years, Nick came to see the white space as silence. Not every feeling can be expressed in words. He did not write the book like he would typically write a philosophical book. He did not examine grief in a detached, scholarly manner. He simply described his feelings.

"The words just came to me," he said. He wrote in pictures—one of the most memorable lines is: "Sorrow is no longer the islands but the sea." He resolved not to include any pious platitudes or false reassurances, only his absolute honest feelings.

"I initially thought there was something unique about me, because I had lost a child," Nick said. "But I soon learned I had a lot of company on the mourner's bench." Since the publication of the book, he's heard from hundreds and hundreds of grieving parents. The circle soon widened to include people who had experienced loss of any kind. "I shall never forget," he said, "a woman in a church who said to me, 'My loss is that my son will never become what I hoped he would be.' I never saw her again, or learned what was behind her comment. But somehow the book spoke to her."

One day, Nick ran into a friend in an airport who was reading *Lament*. "This man, a prominent businessman, had experienced no tragic loss that I knew of. I asked why he was reading my book and he said that he was rereading it after giving copies to all four of his children. I wondered why and he said, 'Don't you see, Nick, that it's a love song?' I suppose it is."

Nick initially wrote as his own therapeutic exercise. As time passed, he began to think his thoughts might be helpful to others. "I began to wonder," he said, "if there might be something redemptive in it, if what I was writing might somehow make something redemptive out of this experience. I resolved not to disown my grief, but to seek to own it redemptively—own it in such a way that might bring about some good."

Henri Nouwen was among those who praised *Lament*, writing, "This little book is a true gift to those who grieve and those who, in love, reach out to comfort. Wolterstorff's words are, indeed, 'salve on our wounds.' Thank God he did not remain silent."

Still, Nick had doubts. He happened to be at the printing plant of the William B. Eerdmans Co., the book's publisher, and saw a pallet with hundreds of copies of *Lament for a Son* stacked on it, in preparation for shipping. An image came to him: He saw himself lying flat, in a casket or on a stretcher, with his intestines exposed, as people filed past gawking at him. What had he done?

∾

Despite his initial misgivings, the book became one of the most popular pastoral theology books ever published by Eerdmans. It has sold exponentially more than Nick's many volumes on philosophy.

As time has passed, Nick has thought deeply about what grief is, about God's relationship to those who are suffering, and about death. In 2012, he spoke on "Befriending the Grieving," to hospital chaplains in Dallas and in 2016 on "Living with Grief" at the Mayo Clinic. Many of his thoughts on the nature of grief were included in a chapter entitled "Living with Grief" in his memoir *In This World of Wonders*, published in 2019. Over the years he concluded that grief is rooted in love, particularly "attachment" love. Attachment love is different than the love we feel for things like music or art that attract us, and different from the love we feel for activities like gardening or playing the piano. Attachment love is a deeper, more mysterious love that desires the well-being and flourishing of the beloved. Grief occurs when the object of one's attachment dies, disappears, or is destroyed. Grief wants the impossible—it wants the lost loved one back. Thus grief wants what has been done to be undone while simultaneously knowing that that cannot happen. In this way, grief is not rational. But it is not pathological, though it may become pathological. For example, Nick told me of a lawyer he knew who lost a child and went back to work one week later. "The man was an emotional wreck," he said. But grief is not necessarily pathological. Instead, Nick sees grief as admirable, saying that if your child was worth loving when alive, then he or she is worth grieving over when dead.

Western society is fixated on what Nick calls "disowning" grief. He points out the language we use: "put it behind you," "get over it" and "get on with your life" as language of disowning. The goal of grieving is not to move on from it, to somehow overcome it, the goal is to own it and take it in to your being. As time passes, the goal shifts from not only owning one's grief, but owning it redemptively, to use it to help others. Surely this is what Frederick Buechner means by the phrase "the stewardship of pain."

Much has been written about the stages of grief, with grief being described as a process one goes through with the end result that one can move on to the rest of one's life. Nick rejects those ideas. "I used to have people come to see me in my office," he said, "who had experienced loss and were frustrated because they weren't experiencing the stages of grief. They thought something was wrong with them. There wasn't anything wrong with them other than believing that grief comes in stages."

∾

I read a few lines to Nick from something I had found online instructing preachers in how to talk to their congregations about suffering. The gist of it was that suffering and death are tools God uses to shape and mold us. The article spoke about meekly submitting to the rod of the Father and being quiet under God's smiting rod because it is training for holiness. Although the language of this particular article seemed archaic and extreme, there is a Christian tradition of viewing suffering as God's tool for soul-making, and I asked Nick what he thought of that.

"I find it grotesque and repugnant," he said sharply. "What did Eric's untimely death do for his soul? And the idea that God would cause Eric's foot to slip for my moral and religious improvement is grotesque. I may have grown deeper through my suffering, but to suggest that God employs the death of children to improve their parents is repugnant."

Forty years after Eric's death, Nick still grieves for his son. The pain is not as intense, but it remains. "The hole never closes," he said. "You repair it, but it does not close completely. How could it? Am I supposed to forget Eric?"

∾

I first read *Lament for a Son* in the late 1980s, not long after it was published. One of my takeaways was the assertion that God is appalled by death. Nick writes that the biblical view is not that death is something God uses for our good: "The Bible speaks instead of God's overcoming death. Paul calls it the last great enemy to be overcome. ... My pain over my son's death is shared by his pain over my son's death. And, yes, I share in his pain over his son's death."

As the book goes on, my impression is that Nick writes more philosophically and theologically. He confirmed this, noting that the final pages reflect his thinking several months after Eric's death.

Toward the end of the book, Nick writes about the pathos of God. He writes that he had long known God was not the impassive being historically portrayed by theologians. What his grief brought into focus was the suffering of God. God was not just the God of those who suffer, but the God who suffers. "Through the prism of my tears," he writes, "I have seen a suffering God."

Words like "impassive" and "pathos" lead into the realm of philosophers and theologians. Divine impassability is the idea that God does not experience emotions and is immune from pain and pleasure. This has been doctrine in the church over the centuries. Proponents of this view argue that an emotional God becomes subject to other beings and, therefore, cannot be God. Nick rejects divine impassibility, saying its origins are found not in the Bible but in the writings of the first century Greek philosopher Plotinus.

Divine pathos ascribes a full range of human emotion to God. Perhaps most forcefully articulated by Abraham Joshua Heschel in his classic work *The Prophets*, divine pathos draws from scriptures that speak of God's delight, God's anger, and God changing his mind. Heschel writes: "The voice of God calling upon the people to weep, lament, and mourn, for the calamities are about to descend upon them, is itself a voice of grief, a voice of weeping."

"Instead of explaining our suffering," Nick writes, "God shares it."

Knowing that his views on divine impassibility and divine pathos have not changed over the decades, I asked Nick how his view of God has changed since Eric's death. "Before Eric's accident," he said, "my God was too domesticated. God is much more mysterious than I imagined."

Decades later, he would write in his memoir, "I still trust God; but I no longer trust God to protect me and my family from harm and grief." He wrote then that perhaps if Eric had not died, he would have taken up the philosophical and theological challenge of the problem of evil. But such an exercise did not appeal to him given what he had experienced.

He explained his reservations in his memoir: "I could not bring myself to try to figure out what God was up to in Eric's death. I joined the psalmist in lamenting without explaining. Things have gone awry in God's world. I do not understand why, nor do I understand why God puts up with it for so long. Rather than Eric's death evoking in me an interest in theodicy, it had the effect of making God more mysterious. I live with the mystery."

Nick maintains God's ultimate desire for humanity is best expressed by the word "shalom." Although often thought of as meaning peace, shalom means more than that, along the lines of the famous remark of Martin Luther King Jr.: "True peace is not the absence of tension, but the presence of justice."

Nick says the best word to describe shalom may be 'flourishing'.

I asked then what the relationship is between grief and shalom.

"Many things upset and rupture shalom," Nick said, "and God is sad about those things. The death of a child upsets the order of shalom. It's wrong. Eric was supposed to bury me, not the other way around. Grief is a breach in shalom. Grief is incompatible with full shalom. As one learns to live around the gap in one's life that grief represents, and as one learns to own one's grief redemptively, there's a healing of the breach. But the fact that grief never fully disappears means that, in this life, the healing of the breach of shalom is never complete."

～

A few years ago, Nick was invited to participate in what turned out to be one of the most impactful teaching experiences of his life. Calvin University had established a new campus inside the Handlon State Prison for Men outside of Iona, Michigan, about 25 miles east of the main campus. Some inmates at Handlon are full Calvin students, earning bachelor's degrees. *Lament for a Son* had been assigned as a textbook in an introduction to philosophy course and Nick entered the prison to discuss the book. Seventeen of the twenty inmates in the class were serving life sentences. The inmates read passages from the book aloud and spoke of how it gave words to what they felt.

"They confessed what they had done," Nick said. "One would say, 'I killed my best friend,' and another 'I murdered my wife,' and so on. I had never experienced anything like it. I came to see that prisons are houses of lament, houses of grief. I felt my common humanity with these men profoundly." Nick returns to the prison annually to discuss the book.

In his 90s, Nicholas Wolterstorff thinks about his own death. There are things he'd like to say to Eric, but he does not claim to know how God's new creation will work. "I have no idea," he said. "There are billions of people for God to deal with. I think about what's next, but I do not know what's going to happen. It is a mystery."

In the months following Eric's death, Nick found comfort in rereading T.S. Eliot's *Four Quartets*, and was especially struck by the line "In my end is my beginning." Nick also found resonance with John Donne's sentiment that "Any man's death diminishes me, because I am involved in mankind." The paradox and mystery of "In my end is my beginning," parallels the paradox and mystery of owning grief and making it redemptive. And if any death diminishes, how much more the death of a beloved child?

Nick was indeed wounded by the loss of Eric, but through *Lament for a Son* and his willingness to speak over the decades of his particular experience of grief, Nicholas Wolterstorff has been an agent of love, compassion, and mercy in our broken and battered world. At the end of *Lament*, he notes, "That the radiance which emerges from acquaintance with grief is a blessing to others is familiar, though perplexing: How can we treasure the radiance while struggling against what brought it about? How can we thank God for suffering's yield while asking for its removal?"

Until that day when God wipes every tear from our eyes, when mourning and crying and pain are no more, and death is no more, we live in the mystery.

∾

I thought long and hard about who to invite to comment on Nicholas Wolterstorff's story. I wondered who had the stature. I was reticent to invite another philosopher or theologian—I feared I might wind up refereeing a debate about divine impassibility versus divine pathos. I actually said to myself, "I've got to think creatively about this," and the word "creative" brought to mind a creative person: Makoto Fujimura.

Mako is a visual artist who has lived, worked, and studied in both Japan and the United States, and his paintings have been exhibited worldwide. He is also a deep thinker who has written several books about the intersections (and sometimes collisions) between the worlds of art and faith. I was not surprised to learn that Mako and Nick know each other, or that Nick, an art collector, owns a couple of Mako's paintings. They were very comfortable being paired in this book.

"I probably first read *Lament for a Son* close to thirty years ago," Mako said. "Then, after I experienced the trauma of 9/11 firsthand, my pastor gave *Lament* to me and I read it again. Someone else gave it to me a while ago after I went through a divorce. So I read it again. People keep giving it to me. I'm not sure how many times I have read it—maybe five, and I've also given several copies to people suffering pain or trauma or unexpected loss. Nick's words are powerful and intimate and speak more clearly than any discourse on pain or loss.

"Yet I am not sure *Lament for a Son* was my first exposure to Nick. I read his book *Art in Action* in the 1990s, and we met when we participated in an academic conference together. I appreciate Nick's approach to art. Not only is he a great philosopher, but he is also a fine carpenter—he is from generations of people who used their hands to build their homes and furniture. His understanding of art as making is somatic and, although he is a very high level thinker, he translates philosophy to a deeply communal level, which is very helpful to someone like me, who navigates both an art world that is disembodied and even gnostic, and a church world that can be gnostic as well, when we lean into super-rationalized ways of understanding the gospel as information only. I don't fit into the machinations of either of those worlds. I often experience being marginalized. I am not alone—many creatives are marginalized. Nick brings an important connection between work with hands and art, and speaks powerfully to us."

≈

Creativity and the act of creation, according to Mako, are "gratuitous." I tend to hear that word negatively, usually in reference to gratuitous violence or gratuitous sex in a movie. Yet if we suspend the negative connotation, and simply hold onto gratuitous meaning unnecessary, it opens new windows into the nature of God. Creation is unnecessary in the sense that although God is by nature creative, God does not need to create. Instead, God chooses to create out of love. Creation, Mako writes, is a "superfluous act of generosity." Part of the mystery of creation is that what seems superfluous or unnecessary is actually vital. In God's upside-down economy, where the last are first and first last, the stone the builders rejected becomes the cornerstone. What is viewed as useless or unnecessary in the eyes of the world is crucial in the kingdom of God.

Art is not useful or utilitarian. In an industrialized world of production, artists are easily overlooked. There is a long list of great artists, like Vincent Van Gogh and Emily Dickinson, who were ignored during their lifetimes. "Could it be," Mako asks, "that what is deemed marginal, what is 'useless' in our terms, is most essential for God and is the bedrock, the essence, of our culture?"

"Similarly, *Lament for a Son* is a gratuitous act of generosity," Mako said, "drawn from Nick's experience. It breaks categorical realities of academia and publishing. It is not a book of philosophy, but it is written by a great philosopher. It wasn't useful or necessary for Nick's career as a philosopher, but it is an essential book and is the book of his that has reached the widest audience. I am sure he made a costly sacrifice writing this book. No wonder he had that moment of seeing himself exposed and wondering what he had done when he saw copies of the book stacked up to be shipped. I know from personal experience that it is difficult to write about your own pain and trauma. Writing can help, but it also hurts. While it can be healing to put things down on paper, it's also re-traumatizing as you relive painful events. You are writing about things you wish had never happened and you feel the weight of them over and over.

"This must have been hard for someone who is as deep a thinker as Nick is. His deep capacity for thought makes me appreciate his approach even more. He does not ask, 'Why did my son die?' or enter into philosophical questions, which he is very capable of doing. Instead, he speaks straight from the heart. I see strong parallels with a verse that means a lot to me, John 11:35: 'Jesus wept.' The context of that verse is the death of Lazarus and the grief of his sisters Mary and Martha. Why would Jesus weep when he had the power to resurrect Lazarus? He knows he can fix the problem. And he could have come to them earlier, when he first heard Lazarus was sick, and healed him and avoided the pain altogether. Instead, Jesus chooses to enter into the pain and then chooses to stay in the lament. He stayed in the tears and grief of Mary and Martha and the community that was suffering. It's exactly the right thing to do, but Jesus didn't have to do it."

In his 2020 book *Art and Faith*, Mako writes: "'Jesus wept' gives us a perspective on God's gratuitous compassion, and it highlights intuition and creativity as entry points into God's Word. ... More and more I am drawn to see all of scripture through this lens. We are used to hearing the Christian gospel as a victorious message, but when viewed ... through Christ's tears, that gospel may appear a bit 'upside down.' We are told that by following Christ, everything will be restored; in some cases, we are promised prosperity. Church programs seem to be dedicated to helping us improve our lives, have better marriages, and become better parents. All of these good outcomes are not against God's design for abundance in the world, but John 11:35 adds to the complexity of this version of the Good News."

Certainly the incarnate Christ experienced the full range of human emotions. His tears, shed for our brokenness and pain, were also shed at the loss of Eric Wolterstorff. Japanese culture is more attuned to seeing this type of beauty than Western culture. The Japanese aesthetic of *wabi-sabi* sees beauty in what is well-worn, used, and even broken. The Japanese phrase *mono no aware* describes the fleeting beauty and the pathos of things wearing away. "Jesus wept" is an expression of divine pathos that fits these sensibilities.

Seeing how important pathos is to Eastern culture, I am left to conclude that divine impassibility is a doctrine that could only have risen in the West.

∽

Early on the morning of September 11, 2001, Mako left his loft apartment in southern Manhattan, three blocks away from the World Trade Center. His children were in school that morning in the shadow of the Twin Towers. After the attacks, Mako searched for hours to find his family. His subway train had to backtrack to avoid disaster, and while in the subway he felt the rumble of the first tower falling overhead. The subway train backtracked for two miles; when Mako exited the subway, the Twin Towers were gone.

"I thought I lost my children that day," Mako said. "To say it was traumatic is a great understatement. My family witnessed the devastation, and my children are 'Ground Zero' children. We saw that smoldering hole for months and looked out at Ground Zero for the next decade until we moved from that place. The amount of loss—in New York, Pennsylvania, and Washington, D.C.—is incalculable. 9/11 pushed me over the edge. In the months that followed, T.S. Eliot's *Four Quartets*, the same poems Nick turned to after the death of his son, became my guidebook. It became my map to navigate a really confusing time.

"Eliot's *Four Quartets* is the consummation of everything Eliot had ever written. He was so satisfied with *Four Quartets* that he did not write another poem—it was the end of poetry for him. Some of the sections of the poems are dark—they are really the nadir of Western poetry. When you go through darkness, as I did following 9/11, Eliot made absolutely the right sense to me. He spoke clearly to the darkness I was going through. It's apparent he also spoke to Nick. Eliot pushes the boundaries of hope, and the fact that Nick could conclude *Lament for a Son* with Eliot's line from the *Four Quartets*, 'In my end is my beginning,' is extraordinarily hopeful. It's an amazing statement of faith to end with that line. It takes an enormous level of self-understanding and honesty to move through the purgatorial fires of pain, to move away from disaffection and distraction, and get to the other side. Eliot's poem does that; Nick does that by being brutally honest about the pain and then, like Eliot, expressing hope that isn't simply a projection, hope that doesn't deny or lose the immediacy of the moment."

∽

In addition to painting, Mako also practices the Japanese art of kintsugi. Kintsugi masters repair ceramics used in Japanese tea ceremonies. "Kin" means gold, and "tsugi" means to mend or reconnect. Using Japanese lacquer and gold to repair cracks and fractures, kintsugi masters do not just repair or restore broken tea ware, they create something new. Ceramic bowls which may have previously had a uniform, indistinguishable appearance are transformed. After the kintsugi process, they are all unique, since no two pieces of ceramic break in the same way.

"Kintsugi is an art form akin to the theology of new creation," Mako said, "that is so prevalent in the New Testament. After trauma—to a bowl or a person—you can never return to the way things were. But something new can be created. Think of Jesus' post-resurrection appearances. These are new creation moments.

It's amazing that after all he suffered he came back as a human being—he could have been anything! Yet he came back as not only a human, but a wounded human. He wasn't the same—people didn't recognize him immediately. This is the unimaginable reality of the new creation because miraculously, somehow, through those wounds we are healed.

"A kintsugi master does not start from the mindset of, 'Oh, this is broken, let's fix it.' A kintsugi master will behold the fragment and say, 'This fragment is enough.' In that moment they name and appreciate the fragment and may not even think of mending it for a while. It is a singular piece, and we can find beauty in that piece. We see in kintsugi a process of looking at the brokenness, beholding it, naming the fractures, finding them beautiful, and then mending in a way that accentuates the fractures instead of hiding them. Something new is created. Gold is poured in and the new design is completely dependent upon the wounds. You could say of kintsugi, 'In my end is my beginning.' What was broken is made into something new that can be used again. This is a profound message for us in the West. In the West, we quickly discard what is broken. When we seek to do kintsugi in the United States, nobody has broken ceramics. They've already been thrown away."

In addition to meaning to mend or reconnect, "tsugi" also can mean connecting to the next generation.

"The connotation of kintsugi meaning 'to pass to the next generation' is appropriate and poignant when thinking about Nick," Mako said. "What does it mean to be a father when the absence of your son is so painfully real? Sometimes a kintsugi master will not mend a bowl. Instead, the fragments are passed to the next generation, along with the story of who the bowl served and how it was broken. I have a Korean bowl that was taken to Japan and was used in high tea. It was made in the 17th century and broke in the 18th century. The fragments were held for two generations before it was given to a kintsugi master to mend, and it was mended in the 19th century. There's a lesson in that—some trauma is not possible to mend right away—it takes generations. Think of the Columbine High School families, or the 9/11 families, or the survivors of countless other ground zeroes around the world. Sometimes all we can do is tenderly pass the fragments down.

"In this way, what Nick is doing in *Lament for a Son* is very Eastern. If he had wanted to argue his way into suffering, he has the mind—maybe the best mind—to do that. But he chose not to. Instead, he beheld and named his emptiness—using the white space on the page to express that. His book is written like a haiku—sparse, beautifully descriptive, and beautifully written."

As Mako spoke about creating something more beautiful from broken pieces through doing kintsugi, I thought of a line from William Butler Yeats' poem "Crazy Jane Talks to the Bishop":

Nothing can be sole or whole
that has not been rent.

Kintsugi is that sort of bridge from creation to new creation.

"You cannot undo the past," Mako said, "but you can mend it to make something new. That's the shift towards a kintsugi life. A kintsugi life embodies the idea of the stewardship of pain. People experience healing in our kintsugi workshops. Our culture doesn't have language for lament, yet everyone has some sort of trauma—for example, we've all been traumatized by the pandemic. After 2020 and 2021, we're all survivors. Our kintsugi workshops have revealed that giving people simple devices—and if they don't have something broken, we give them shells—to work with is healing. They fill the cracks with putty, then sand it, and add gold, and it comes out beautiful, even the first time. Trauma therapists have told us that brain neurons get rewired as a person does the physical act of kintsugi. They have said that it may take them six months of talk therapy to get to where our kintsugi workshops go in two hours. Something is awakened that our Western society, with its utilitarian and industrialized realities, has lost. We create space where it is safe to play and use your hands. Simply sanding for a long time, and listening to sandpaper go over putty and ceramic, is enormously healing. In our consumerist society, we do all sorts of things to numb pain. But once you give people language and a way to redirect pain that's been suppressed, beautiful things happen.

"I spent the 20th anniversary of 9/11 doing kintsugi. I felt I could not go back down to Ground Zero. I'm not over 9/11; I'm still going through it. Major pieces may have been restored, but there are still hairline fractures. I'm grateful my children are doing well and they were at Ground Zero for the 20th anniversary. That says a lot about their resilience. They went with their friends, and it's beautiful to see ways the next generation may have strength I don't have. The weight of being a Ground Zero parent is enormous, yet the only way forward is to move into the pain.

"Similarly, I can imagine ways in which it was healing for Nick to put *Lament for a Son* together. He assembled the book like a fine carpenter working his craft—focusing on details and not trying to do everything at once. His micro-focus is like sanding the pieces of kintsugi. At that particular place, during a particular time, in a particular way, Nick was dealing with his pain. He does not make grandiose philosophical statements—he doesn't go macro. Like a good craftsman, he stays in the micro. His honest grappling led him to a certain kind of understanding of his own craft. Writing that book led him, in some ways, to the gold. He is a good steward of his pain because of his craftsman's dedication to paying attention and telling the truth of what he experienced. Because he did this, others can easily connect with what he's done. His discipline as both a philosopher and craftsman allowed him to do something very difficult—to both experience the pain and at the same time tell us about it. That's very hard to do while you're in the middle of it.

"The final test of any work is, 'Is it generative?' Does it give birth in the reader's mind and life? A work that does this is a rare gift, and *Lament for a Son* does this. It is a book that endures. He didn't write the book and say, 'I'm all better now.' Instead, he's lovingly and carefully holding the fragments and passing them on."

Nicholas Wolterstorff is Noah Porter Emeritus Professor of Philosophical Theology at Yale University. www.Wikipedia.org/wiki/ Nicholas_Wolterstorff

Makoto Fujimura is an internationally acclaimed artist and writer based in Princeton, New Jersey. www.MakotoFujimura.com

The Thing with Feathers

"Hope is the thing with feathers
That perches in the soul,
And sings the tune without the words,
And never stops at all."

Emily Dickinson

Several years ago, when I was working in youth ministry, I was helping out at a camp in Northern Michigan. We had been doing an activity at night in the woods, and after it was over, I stayed with the person cleaning up. We loaded all the gear—including at least a dozen lanterns—into the bed of an all-terrain cart, but there was so much stuff we filled the passenger seat as well.

"Go ahead," I said to my companion. "I'll just walk back."

It wasn't until he drove away that I realized I had made a mistake.

I was alone in the woods in absolute, utter, complete darkness. It was an overcast night and there was no moon, and since my cell phone didn't have a signal out there, I had not brought it and its built-in flashlight with me. Once the taillights of the maintenance cart disappeared, I was alone in the dark. I put my hand in front of my face and waved it, just to see if that cliché was true. It was. I could not see the hand in front of my face. In a matter of seconds, I lost the trail and was plodding into the underbrush, hoping not to walk into a tree or step into a hole or wake an animal better left sleeping. The land was hilly, and I knew if I wasn't careful, I would wind up falling down a slope. I knew the right direction to walk, but what if I got turned around?

As I was thinking about that, I found a big spider web with my face. It's hard to stay calm with a spider web on your face. And then I heard rustling sounds around me. It's even harder to stay calm when you are alone in the dark with a spider web on your face hearing rustling sounds around you. I was hoping those noises were being made by squirrels or chipmunks and not bears or wolves. That was only the beginning of the wildlife possibilities. I'd seen wild turkeys going up into the trees to roost at night—what would happen if I disturbed one of them? Wild turkeys can be maniacal when backed into a corner. Plus, there were deer everywhere in these woods—what if one of them came at me with its antlers? The overwhelming temptation was to just sit down and wait for the morning. Maybe I could tough it out—the sun would rise in another eight hours. I wondered how long it would be before anyone noticed I was gone.

I didn't sit down. Instead, I just kept putting one foot in front of the other. What should have been at most a ten-minute hike took the better part of an hour. I walked into camp with spider web silk in my hair and burrs on my clothes. I felt like someone should kill a fatted calf for me, for I was lost and now was found—yet my return was anticlimactic, my wife didn't even know I was lost, she simply thought I was elsewhere in camp, attending to other things.

I have thought often about that experience as I've done the interviews in this book. Putting one foot in front of the other to keep going even though you're in the dark is an easy metaphor for facing traumatic loss. How did Roger, Quentin, Rosemerry, Nick, and the others do it? How did they find the strength not to just sit down but instead keep going even when they couldn't see the way in front of them?

~

T.S. Eliot's *Four Quartets*, which has been referred to in the pages of this book, has a line in it that says, "Old men should be explorers." I have found, as I enter my mid-60s, much encouragement and profound wisdom from exploring these stories. Each interview—both with the people whose stories I told and with those who helped me process the stories—has stuck with me. I find myself thinking about them often and have learned so many things about life from them. I've also learned some things about death.

Death became omnipresent during the pandemic years. Of course, death is always with us, but we usually keep it at arm's length through denial and inattention. The pandemic focused our thinking—as millions died worldwide, every one of us left wondered if the pandemic might bring our demise. A sore throat or runny nose would get me thinking if I was ready to die.

How should we think about death?

Nicholas Wolterstorff, echoing the Apostle Paul, called death "the great enemy." Death ends relationships, and ends life, which God called "very good." Death is the ultimate outrage. Ron Nelson, Quiniece Henry, Sandie Kinsinger, Finn Trommer, and Eric Wolterstorff—like countless others—should have lived longer.

Dylan Thomas wrote of raging against the dying light, but one wonders what good it would do. Our enemy does not fight fair. It's estimated 117 billion people have lived in the history in the world. Death's won-loss record is 117,000,000,000 to 0.

Not all of us experience death as an enemy. When someone is suffering, like my mother in the grip of unrelenting Alzheimer's, death doesn't seem like the enemy. It comes as a friend. Anne Lamott writes, with her typical humor, "Death is not the enemy. Snakes are." She continues, speaking of death as it comes to those who have lived long lives: "Somehow, as we get older, death becomes as sacred as birth, and while we don't exactly welcome it, death becomes a friend."

The point she eventually goes on to make is that, although we have a fear of death instilled in us from childhood, death is actually a transition to a new life and as such is not to be feared. I feel a poignant paradox here: Death is both enemy and friend.

Frederick Buechner wrote a beautiful meditation on dying that speaks of death as a transition. Like many, Buechner was afraid of flying. In *Beyond Words: Daily Readings in the ABC's of Faith*, he starts by imagining being on an airplane.

He describes the agonizing moments as an anxious passenger warily eyes the flight attendants, listens to all the ominous sounds as the plane taxis and guns its engines, feels the vibrations of rumbling along the tarmac and the surge upwards into the air—until finally the plane breaks through a sea of clouds to a clear sky. Then, he concludes:

"Possibly the last takeoff of all is something like that. When the time finally comes, you're scared stiff to be sure, but maybe by then you're just as glad to leave the whole show behind and get going. In a matter of moments, everything that seemed to matter stops mattering. The slow climb is all there is. The stillness. The clouds. Then the miracle of flight as from fathom upon fathom down you surface suddenly into open sky. The dazzling sun."

I find comfort and hope in those images. As I think of the people whose stories I've told, I see hope and resilience as threads that hold them together. One of the places their resilience comes from is the hope that death is not the last word, but a transition to something else, something beautiful beyond our imaginations.

"Hope is the thing with feathers," Emily Dickinson famously wrote, "that perches in the soul." She goes on in that poem to speak of hope as a bird that doesn't stop singing, regardless of storms and gales.

I love that image. Hope, like a songbird, perseveres, regardless of life's storms and gales. It is resilient. And, like Buechner's airplane, it has wings.

The people whose stories are told in this book all remain hopeful, despite the worst happening. Hope does not ignore reality. In their own ways, the people featured in this book put into practice the words of Wendell Berry: "Be joyful though you have considered all the facts." Those words come from Berry's poem "Manifesto," and Berry ends that poem saying, "Practice resurrection," which is another thing the people featured in this book do.

∽

In an earlier chapter, Chuck DeGroat said that resilience comes as we live out of our True Self. I see that being lived out in the stories told in this book. Untimely deaths rip the fabric of shalom, our sense of wholeness. The wounds will never go away. But how do we "make this wound our medicine?" There are no easy paths or quick fixes. Over and over, the people in these pages speak of life-giving practices they've engaged in: therapy, poetry, kintsugi, time away, and classic spiritual disciplines like prayer and contemplation.

Yet there is something else, something Nicholas Wolterstorff speaks of at the end of *Lament for a Son*: "The valley of suffering is the vale of soul-making." Each of the people whose stories are told would not be who they are without the crucible of the tragic events they've experienced. In each case, the worst has happened, and they are better for it. Each would trade how they've grown in an instant to have their loved one back. Each rejects the idea that God would kill their loved one to somehow improve them. Yet they all have become wiser, deeper, and more fully human.

Ultimately, resilience comes from the experience of community. When tragedy strikes, many of us have an impulse to move away, perhaps out of fear. But what matters are those who we move toward. Mitch Kinsinger, absorbed in grief and his own recovery from his stem cell transplant, was buoyed by phone calls and text messages. Decades after his father's murder, Roger Nelson remembers friends who drove from Michigan to Iowa for the funeral and gathered for a spaghetti dinner. Quentin Henry remembers even those who said the wrong thing with affection (and let's face it, the fear of saying the wrong thing paralyzes many of us). He knew their hearts were in the right place. Rosemerry Trommer consoled the father of a boy who had shunned her son, but also drew strength from the man's expression of sympathy.

We never figure everything out in isolation, we need others around us.

～

When I worked for Western Theological Seminary, I was out in California making calls with the seminary president. At the end of a very long day, we visited an older man named Frank. His wife was out, the sun was setting, and it was obvious Frank was sitting in the late afternoon gloom crying. We asked what was wrong, and Frank took us into a back bedroom and showed us a picture of his son, Frank Jr., who had killed himself a few years earlier.

"I'm just sitting here thinking about my son," Frank said. Our eyes filled with tears, too. It was such a sad scene. What can be said or done in the face of such sadness? We just sat in the dark with

Frank. We had planned to spend fifteen or twenty minutes with him, but wound up being there over an hour, until his wife came home. After we left, we drove the first half an hour or so in silence, feeling the weight of Frank's grief.

Sometimes the only answer is to sit in the dark with someone.

As we sit, we often remember.

As we remember, we recall stories we might wish to tell.

And that healthy instinct—if we are honest as Buechner urges us repeatedly to be—can help us bypass a forest of theological arguments to reach toward a compassionate connection with ourselves and our loved ones.

What came clear to me as I worked on this book is that as much as throughout my career I have held up theology as essential, there is so much bad theology out there about why traumatic events happen and what God is supposedly accomplishing through these events that I believe we've reached a tipping point where we just need to keep our mouths shut and simply love people instead of offering explanations for the unexplainable.

I go back to what our old professor told Roger Nelson about the agonizing death of the professor's son: Even if God were to write down the reasons why this awful loss had happened, our professor would wad up the paper and throw it back in God's face. Real people need compassion and empathy, not our explanations. Besides, God doesn't need a defense attorney. Pastoral considerations often should take precedence over theological positions. I wish everyone putting forward those positions could see the fire in Nick Wolterstorff's eyes and hear the pain in his voice when he calls those positions grotesque and repugnant.

Something is strangely out of whack when theological pronouncements further wound already suffering people.

$\sim$

Talking with Nick helped me see more clearly what the "stewardship of pain" entails. In a world fixated on disowning grief, the challenge is to open oneself to grief, to own it, and then, ultimately, to own it redemptively. Nick owned his grief by writing *Lament for a Son,* and that book has helped countless others. Roger Nelson has owned his grief in countless pastoral encounters and in his preaching, the depth of which is borne out of his experience of trauma. Quentin Henry has owned his grief by telling the story of Quiniece's horrific death. Mitch Kinsinger's experience with traumatic loss led him to change careers and live with a focused sense of life's fleeting nature. Rosemerry Trommer didn't shy away from meeting Finn's suicide with remarkable openness, and her poems of grief speak to large audiences.

The other day, I came across this in a book by a respected Christian author: "A well-known minister, after his wife passed away, said he had to learn that there is a difference between turning loose your loved one and turning loose your grief. You will always hold your loved one in your heart, but you must let go of your grief. So far as possible, we must walk away from painful and destructive feelings. Simply that. Walk away."

I wrote "NO!!!" in huge letters in the margin of my book.

To be fair to the author, I think what he was trying to say was "don't get stuck in your pain," as Frederick Buechner so eloquently writes in his essay "Adolescence and the Stewardship of Pain," which started me on this whole project. Don't be Miss Havisham, from Dickens' *Great Expectations,* moldering away in her wedding dress after being jilted at the altar. Unfortunately, that's not how the point comes across in that book I was reading. To me, those words were "Christian" encouragement to disown grief, which I wholeheartedly reject. Labeling grief a destructive feeling is inexcusable. Grief, as Nick explains, is not pathological. There is nothing wrong with it and it is not something to walk away from or turn loose or get over or put away.

The damage done by the suggestion we must flee feelings of sadness, grief, and pain is incalculable. The church can do better than that. We can be a community that honors grief amid a culture of denial. Even if a feeling seems "negative," we're better off recognizing and accepting the full range of human emotion and experience—including grief—than trying to banish our feelings.

The way forward is never around but always through.

Dan Rooks' vision, early in this book, is a vision for what we can be—communities that encourage their members to love fully and suffer well. Roger Nelson, Quentin Henry, Mitch Kinsinger, Rosemerry Trommer, and Nicholas Wolterstorff have all done that. I'm indebted to Roger, Quentin, Mitch, Rosemerry, and Nick for sharing their stories with me. Similarly, the wisdom and insight shared by Dan Rooks, Marilyn McEntyre, Mary Anderson, Suzanne McDonald, Chuck DeGroat, Sophie Mathonnet-VanderWell, and Makoto Fujimura have helped me process the stories.

This is mysterious, paradoxical work.

Nick wrote, "The radiance which emerges from acquaintance with grief is familiar, though perplexing: How can we treasure the radiance while struggling against what brought it about? How can we thank God for suffering's yield while asking for its removal?"

As Desmond Tutu said: I don't know the answers but am grateful for the chance to tell these stories.

Care to Read More?

Some of these are books I read while I was researching this one, some are referenced in the previous chapters, some are by the authors I interviewed for this book—and some are just plain good books you may find helpful.

First, if you want to read one additional book, I hope it would be this one: Nicholas Wolterstorff, *Lament for a Son* (Wm. B. Eerdmans Publishing Co., 1987). Small but powerful, this book best demonstrates how to be a good steward of your pain.

After reading *Lament*, if you want to learn more about Nick's remarkable life and career, you can do so here:

Nicholas Wolterstorff, *In This World of Wonders: Memoir of a Life in Learning* (Wm. B. Eerdmans Publishing Co., 2019). There is more about both the initial loss of his son and living with grief here.

If you are interested in learning more about trauma and its after effects, please look at these books:

Bessel van der Kolk, *The Body Keeps the Score: Brain, Mind, and Body in the Healing of Trauma* (Penguin Books, 2014). A classic text on trauma by one of the researchers who first identified PTSD.

Nadine Burke Harris, *The Deepest Well: Healing the Long-Term Effects of Childhood Trauma and Adversity* (Mariner Books, 2018). This book reads like a page-turner detective story as Harris explores the effects of trauma on children.

Remsaa Menakem, *My Grandmother's Hands: Racialized Trauma and the Pathway to Mending our Hearts and Bodies* (Central Recovery Press, 2017). Examines how racialized generational trauma is carried in our bodies.

Here are three compelling first-person accounts of loss and resilience:

J. Todd Billings, *Rejoicing in Lament: Wrestling with Incurable Cancer and Life in Christ* (Brazos Press, 2015). A theologian's thoughts after he was diagnosed with multiple myeloma and endured a stem cell transplant.

Kate Bowler, *Everything Happens for a Reason: and Other Lies I've Loved* (Random House, 2018). The author, a professor of religion who is critical of the Prosperity Gospel, tells her story after being diagnosed with stage IV colon cancer.

Jerry Sittser, *A Grace Disguised: Expanded Edition* (Zondervan, 2004). A professor of religion shares the account of a horrific traffic accident that resulted in the death of his mother, wife, and young daughter.

If you're interested particularly in the theology of loss, which is discussed in this book, these are helpful:

David Carr, *Holy Resilience: The Bible's Traumatic Origins* (Yale University Press, 2014). A scholar of the Hebrew Bible uses trauma theory to go deeper into familiar biblical stories.

C. S. Lewis, *The Problem of Pain* (Macmillan, 1962). This classic contains Lewis' rational and reasoned arguments about what God might be up to when we experience great pain. It should be paired with the next book.

C. S. Lewis, *A Grief Observed* (Seabury Press, 1961). Heartfelt personal reflections after the untimely death of Lewis's wife, the poet Joy Davidman. Lewis does not repudiate his earlier writing, but it is obvious his rational arguments didn't bring him comfort in the face of real loss.

Albert Y. Hsu, *Grieving a Suicide: Revised and Expanded* (InterVarsity Press, 2017). A longtime book editor explores his response to his father's suicide as well as looking at suicide more broadly.

It's not an understatement to say that we live in a culture that denies the reality of death. These books address death (and life) in remarkable ways:

Atul Gawande, *Being Mortal: Medicine and What Matters in the End* (Picador, 2014). A medical doctor on both our acceptance and avoidance of death.

J. Todd Billings, *The End of the Christian Life: How Embracing our Mortality Frees us to Truly Live* (Brazos Press, 2020). As someone living with incurable cancer, Billings reflects on what embracing death teaches us about life.

Marilyn McEntyre, *A Faithful Farewell: Living Your Last Chapter with Love* (Wm. B. Eerdmans Publishing Co., 2015). Meditations written from the point of view of someone facing death.

Marilyn McEntyre, *A Long Letting Go: Meditations on Losing Someone You Love* (Wm. B. Eerdmans Publishing Co., 2015). A companion to *A Faithful Farewell*, these meditations are written from the point of view of the family and friends of someone facing death.

Finally, these book are very much worth exploring:

Frederick Buechner, *Telling Secrets: A Memoir* (HarperSanFrancisco, 1991). The bestselling author and ordained minister shares insightful reflections on his life, including the tragedy of his father's suicide and his daughter's anorexia.

Frederick Buechner, *The Clown in the Belfry: Writings on Faith and Fiction* (HarperSanFrancisco, 1992). A collection of essays that includes "Adolescence and the Stewardship of Pain."

Chuck DeGroat, *When Narcissism Comes to Church: Healing Your Community from Emotional and Spiritual Abuse* (InterVarsity Press, 2020). A psychologist and seminary professor unpacks the effects of narcissism in the church.

Makoto Fujimura, *Art and Faith: A Theology of Making* (Yale University Press, 2020). An artist and deep theological thinker writes about what creativity means. As a Christian, he often feels marginalized by both the world of art and also the church.

Thomas Lynch, *Bone Rosary: New and Selected Poems* (Godine, 2021). A collection of the master poet and undertaker's work. Lynch is a keen observer of life, and his poems contain great wisdom, humor, and insight.

Karen Mulder and Ginger Jurries, *The Compassionate Congregation: A Handbook for People Who Care* (Faith Alive Christian Resources,

2002). A helpful and thorough compilation of resources for helping congregations deal with loss.

Christian Wiman, *My Bright Abyss: Meditation of a Modern Believer* (Farrar, Strauss, and Giroux, 2013). A poet with deep theological insight reflects on the nature of faith. I don't know of another book quite like this one. At the time Wiman was coming to faith, he also was given an incurable cancer diagnosis, yet it isn't cancer that dominates these pages as much as how we can believe in God in this strange world we live in.

Acknowledgments

After I presented on the "stewardship of pain" at an adult education class at a church in my hometown, a woman named Marilyn Bright asked me several penetrating questions about the concept. She spurred me to think deeper. About the same time, my friend Brian Allain said to me, "You should write a book about the stewardship of pain." So I did. Of course that wouldn't have happened without Frederick Buechner sharing that unique combination of words with us in the first place.

No book is written in isolation, especially this one. There would be no book without those who so willingly shared their stories, as well as those who commented on the stories. You've read their names throughout the book and I'm going to repeat them one more time here: Roger Nelson, Dan Rooks, Quentin Henry, Marilyn McEntyre, Mitch Kinsinger, Mary Anderson, Suzanne McDonald, Chuck DeGroat, Rosemerry Wahtola Trommer, Sophie Mathonnet-VanderWell, Nicholas Wolterstorff, and Makoto Fujimura. I am grateful for the gifts of vulnerability and wisdom each gave.

Conversations with Tom and Judy Boogaart, Jack Ridl, and Jon Pott helped steer me and connect me to the people interviewed for this project.

I'm grateful to Karen Mulder, Doug Brouwer, and Jim Gum, who read early drafts of the chapters and gave me helpful feedback. Jeff Crosby did the same with the first draft of the manuscript. I'm grateful to groups at King University in Bristol, Tennessee, Christ Memorial Church and Third Reformed Church in Holland, Michigan, and Thornapple Community Church in Grand Rapids, who listened to different chapters and gave me feedback. I am grateful to Martin Dotterweich, Shari Wolthuis, and Tim Dieffenbach for the invitations to present this material.

I was stuck at one point and Brian Allain helped me again. Brian is a connector, and through Brian I was connected to David Crumm and Front Edge Publishing. I owe a huge debt of gratitude to David and the team at Front Edge.

The decision to not only begin *Reformed Journal Books* but begin it with this project was given a thumbs up by the Reformed Journal board. I'm grateful to Kris DePree, who asked very good questions; Debra Rienstra, who gave wise advice; to my RJ partner Steve Mathonnet-VanderWell, for more than I can list here; to John Hwang, whose quiet competence has helped me and so many others; and to Kerin Beauchamp and Kate Bolt for their endless good energy and enthusiasm. I am grateful too for the role Laurie Orlow plays in our community, along with Rose Postma, Deb Van Duinen, Keith Starkenburg, Mark Hiskes, and Kathy Schoon-Tanis.

Speaking of Mark Hiskes, he helped me put together the discussion guide that you can download to spark individual reflection and group discussion. In the process of doing that, he made a keen grammatical observation that prevented me from embarrassing myself. I am so happy Mark is my friend.

Roger Nelson, Taylor Holbrook, and Harlan Van Oort are life brothers with a special place in my heart. I'm grateful for our ongoing text conversation and the wisdom each of them offers regularly.

My father, Lynn Munroe II, died while this book was in process. I am grateful I was able to explain the concept to him and listen to his advice about where I needed to be careful, yet sad he didn't get to hold the finished product in his hands. He joins the cloud of witnesses and mentors who are no longer here—along with Cliff, Max, Dale, and others—of whom I can say I would not be who I am if I did not know them.

This book would not exist without a special gift from two wonderful and generous people who don't want or seek recognition. I'd tell you more but they don't want me to. Suffice it to say, without them, there's no book.

Finally, I am the lucky guy who gets to be Amanda and Jesse's dad and Gretchen's husband. I find that there aren't words that adequately express the love and admiration I have for each of them. I can imagine them saying, "We agree, but go ahead and try." Okay, here's a feeble effort: You are all courageous (a far different thing from being fearless, you realize there are reasons to be afraid but move ahead anyway). Amanda is wise beyond her years, a friend to so many, and upbeat and energetic. She is often my teacher, and how cool is it as a dad to be able to say that about your child? Jesse is funny, deeply loving of humans and animals, and endlessly patient with his technologically incompetent father. This of course means he too is my teacher, which is still a very cool thing. Gretchen has done what Dan Rooks said, she has "loved fully and suffered well." She doesn't just tolerate my silences and incoherence and endless quirks, she seems to love me in the midst of them. When we were first married, the whole "in sickness and in health" thing applied to her after her stroke. As we age, it's applied to me through cancer and three surgeries in four years. I don't know who I'd be if I had not married her, and I don't want to find out.

Become Part of Our Reformed Journal Community

The *Reformed Journal* is a community of readers and writers who explore faith and life from a generously Reformed perspective. The Reformed tradition is one of the original branches of the Protestant movement with congregations across the U.S. and around the world. The writers who contribute to our online magazine are wise guides—including pastors, professors, and thinkers from various Reformed institutions across the United States and Canada. We stand outside our formal institutional structures to offer free expression.

Although our history dates back to 1951, we have seen a resurgence of activity and interest in our work in recent years. The environmental crisis, racial strife, and political polarization accompanied by fissures in denominational life and shrinking attendance in local congregations have raised many questions about what it means to live a faithful and faith-filled life.

Because of this resurgence in national conversations, in 2024 we launched a book imprint, Reformed Journal Books. In coming years, we hope these books will provide deeper engagement with our writers, providing books that are ideal for individual reflection and small-group discussion.

Please, visit us at our homepage, ReformedJournal.com. Or, you can come directly to ReformedJournal.com/books to learn more about this book and to download a free PDF discussion guide. Through that page you also can contact me about speaking, retreats, or Zoom appearances with discussion groups. Or, you can contact me right now through my website, JeffreyMunroe.com.

Contact info@frontedgepublishing.com to place bulk orders for this book. Bulk orders of Reformed Journal Books can be modified to include information about your group or congregation either on the covers or in additional pages. These modifications make a group read a special opportunity for community outreach.

Finally, book reviews are a great way to let others know about this resource. Please consider writing a book review on the retail platform of your choice or on Goodreads.com.

About the Author

Jeffrey Munroe is editor of the *Reformed Journal*, a digital magazine which explores issues of faith and life from a generously Reformed perspective. He also is the author of *Reading Buechner: Exploring the Work of a Master Memoirist, Novelist, Theologian, and Preacher.* He is a graduate of Michigan State University and Western Theological  Seminary and an ordained minister in the Reformed Church in America. He served in the non-denominational youth ministry Young Life for three decades in West Michigan and Europe, and served as Executive Vice President of Western Theological Seminary for close to a decade. He and his wife Gretchen live in Holland, Michigan, and are the parents of two adult children.

Printed in the USA
CPSIA information can be obtained
at www.ICGtesting.com
CBHW030425080224
4131CB00004B/15

9 781641 801782